Rupert
Just Being Me

Rupert
Just Being Me

Rupert Boneham
as told to Lester Thomas Shane

LifePress is an imprint of Sams Technical Publishing, LLC, 9850 E.30th St., Indianapolis IN 46229.

International Standard Book Number: 0-7906-1331-X

Chief Executive Officer:	Alan Symons
President:	Scott Weaver
Acquisitions Editor:	Brad Schepp
Editorial Assistant:	Heidy Nathan
Pagination Editor:	Kim Heusel
Cover Design:	Mike Walsh
Cover Photos:	Chris Womock

Photos: Provided by Rupert Boneham unless otherwise noted.
Trademark acknowledgments: Where the names of companies, brands, etc are used, the registered trademarks have generally been noted. The companies mentioned in this text in no way endorse the contents of this book, nor have they participated in the publication of this book. All product illustrations, names, and logos are trademarks of their respective manufacturers, including all terms in this book that are known or suspected to be trademarks or service marks. Use of an illustration, term, or logo in this book should not be regarded as affecting the validity of any trademark or service mark, or regarded as an association with or endorsement from the respective trademark holder.

1st Printing

Table of Contents

Dedication

To my wife, Laura, and my daughter, Raya. I can't begin to explain the strength I have seen in you as we traveled through this wonderful and crazy journey. I love you both!

Acknowledgments

I would like to thank my family as well as all of the kids and adults who have come through my world. It is because of all of you that Rupert's Kids is what it is today, and that I am able to write this book.

The Adventure Begins

All adventures have a beginning. Mine officially starts January 27, 1964, in Detroit, Michigan. I may have been born in Motown, but I am definitely not a city kid. By the time I'm three, we move to just outside of Kokomo, Indiana, where my journey really begins.

Kokomo is Small Town, USA. Our first house was actually pretty rural. If you're "outside" of Kokomo, you're really way out in the country. In fact, we were just down the road from a hog farm where we could take corncobs and watermelon rinds and watch the animals literally pig out.

After that we moved around through a few apartments in town until Mom and Dad finally bought the house I grew up in on James Drive. It was a small shotgun kind of place with three little bedrooms, a kitchen, and a living room. The house was comfortably furnished with mostly second-hand stuff acquired

The first shelter I ever built, in Kokomo, Indiana, in 1970. That's me on the right. (Photo by Georgette Boneham)

at Goodwill and the Salvation Army. I remember that everything was in browns and other earth tones.

We moved to Kokomo because my father, Roger F. Boneham, got a job at Indiana University as a professor of geology.

Roger was only 5 feet, 9 inches tall and about 170 pounds, but to me he was a giant. And not a gentle giant. He terrified me. It was not that he was physically abusive, although I got my share of the occasional swats; my dad could destroy me with words and looks. When he wasn't ripping me apart, he was totally indifferent and ignoring me. When I picture my dad at home, he is always sitting alone in his easy chair reading a scientific journal and smoking his pipe or cigars.

*My brother
Christopher and his
monkey, and me.*

Geology was the perfect subject for Roger. Rocks are cold and take millions of years to change.

My relationship with my dad was rocky from the start, and we've never quite smoothed it out.

Roger is who he is. He really didn't have a father to model behavior after. He was raised by grandparents—something he has never made peace with. Over the years he created a mythic Dad with an invented history.

At 10 years old my dad gave me a ring with the initials RFB on it. He said it was given to him when he was a little boy, by his father. He told me how much it meant to him and how proud he was to be able to give it to me.

15

I can still remember the day I lost it at school and how I felt. I also remember the even worse feeling of telling him I had lost it. I found out many years later he didn't know who his father was when he was growing up and the whole story was something he had created. Maybe that's where I learned to create imaginary friends.

My mama, Georgette, was also trained as a scientist and worked as a teacher. She taught chemistry at Lewis Cass High School in Cass County. Every time I run into someone who was in one of Georgette's classes, they tell me that she was the hardest teacher they ever had. She doesn't think she was tough at all. She thought that's how you were supposed to be a teacher. It wasn't that she was trying to be mean; she believed she was doing the right thing and being the best possible teacher she could be. She'll never get why her students didn't necessarily agree.

That's the kind of mom she was. Most of the time she tried really hard to be a mom, but she didn't always know just how to do that. She would read a book on mothering and try some-

The first time I was ever at the Indianapolis 500, with my brother Christopher in 1974. The RFB ring my father gave me is on my finger. (Photo by Roger Boneham)

thing. Unfortunately for her—and for me—not everything can be learned from a book.

Georgette didn't grow up in a loving family either. She was raised with her sister and brother in foster care in Detroit. The foster program must have taught her something about family as they kept her together with her sister. Sadly, her brother was separated from them in the first year.

Her brother, Al, was a neat guy, a psychiatrist up at Northwestern. I liked him a lot. He died when I was about 13.

Her older sister, my Auntie Dollie, was pretty much Georgette's mother figure, and they remained close. But a sister, no matter how loving, isn't a mother, so Georgette never had the model to pattern herself after.

While I was writing this book, my Auntie Dollie had a massive brain hemorrhage and passed away. I will always remember the weeks I would spend with her, Becky, Jimmy, and Uncle Walt as some of my happiest childhood memories.

Georgette is a little lady with a pear-shaped body. She often went on diets but never took any of them very seriously. I inherited both those qualities from my mother. I identified with Mama in many ways. I felt very close to her, and we could play eye contact tag in a crowded room. We always knew exactly where the other one was. To tell the truth, I was pretty much a Mama's boy as a little kid. I even got along better with the girls in the neighborhood and enjoyed playing with my girl cousins.

Chemistry is a science that is all about change. Through chemistry you can create explosions. Just like my relationship with my father has been pretty glacial, Mama and I have experimented with lots of formulas in creating our relationship. Some have worked like magic. Some of them have really blown up in our faces. Some transformed us both for the better. Right now, we are in a really good place with each other, and Georgette Boneham is the chairwoman of the board for my charity, Rupert's Kids.

When I was just over a year old—13 months to be exact, my brother Christopher was born. For me, things went from bad to worse.

At some point, Mama just seemed to disappear. I didn't really know why. Nobody explained that she was going to the hospital to have a baby. I was just suddenly left alone with Roger. When we went to pick up my new brother, the hospital just kept me there. I was suffering from dehydration and malnourishment. Roger really did ignore me a whole lot of the time. Left alone with him he nearly ignored me to death. So my association to the birth of my baby brother is completely linked to feelings of abandonment.

My first memory of actually dealing with Christopher is being behind the house and about to smash his little head in with a brick. Mama interrupted. To me, that was just her playing favorites.

We never really were what you think of as a family, or at least what I imagine a real family to be. I have always wished for a family filled with unconditional love and support. What I got was a world where everything had conditions. It was expected that you were supposed to take care of yourself, not rely on anyone else for anything—ever. We were more like four people who lived together. Roger isolated himself in the living room with his reading and tobacco; Georgette escaped to a bedroom that she converted into her own little sitting room with a TV and radio; my brother and I tolerated each other in the third bedroom. What we shared as a family was our anger, frustration, and disappointments—with the world and with each other.

To be fair, I guess they had reason to be disappointed in me. I'm sure I was not the son they hoped for. I was fat and funny looking. Because of my undiagnosed dyslexia, I must have seemed pretty stupid, too, especially to parents who were scientists, teachers, and scholars.

It was made all the worse, because they could compare me to my brother who always seemed to be better at everything. They encouraged us to be competitive with each other. On the one hand, I was expected to be an older brother who took care of him, the way Auntie Dollie looked after Mama when they were growing up. But Christopher and I were also being told to try and be better than each other. It wasn't very long before he was winning in all areas. I learned that even in this dysfunctional family, I was the loser who didn't fit in.

I didn't fit in with other kids either. In fact, I can't remember having a single friend till about the second grade. I had my imaginary friends. And I had animal buddies. There's a picture of me as a one-year-old cuddled up with a mama cat and her kittens. Even then, at age one, I knew that you could trust animals. I've never met an animal who lied to me, cheated me, or tricked me.

When I was three years old, I was playing in the woods near our old house back in the country. We still had some family friends we would visit, and I had discovered that the woods were the one place—a place without people—where I could fit in.

As a little kid these woods seemed like millions of acres of wilderness with a raging river running through it. In reality, it was probably less than ten acres with a small creek. But it was a world where I could create my whole life. The only rules to obey were those of Nature. Once you learn Mama Nature's rules, she never changes them. She will definitely punish you if you disobey the rules, but that's to teach you the lesson. She gives you a licking for what you've done wrong, not for who you are. She demands respect, but she never gets pissed off for no reason. And she treats everyone and everything the same: you, the plants, the animals, the water, and the sky. She is the ultimate Mama who embraces everything.

So this three-year-old child of nature is playing in his woods catching salamanders and having a great time. Suddenly I catch a glimpse of a tail. It's a snake's tail, and Mr. Snake is buried deep in a fallen log. I remember thinking, "That snake wants to be with me. I need to rescue him."

I never caught a snake before and wasn't sure what to do, so I grab his tail so he wouldn't run away. I definitely don't want to hurt him, but I was afraid that I might scare him and he'd take off. So I hold on.

I spend over an hour digging through the log with my bare little hands, chipping away at the bark all the while holding on to the snake's tail. When I finally get him out, he is, of course, totally freaked. I mean, he was having a quiet day resting in a log, and this strange creature attacked him. So he bites me.

Other kids might have screamed or been frightened. I thought he was trying to hold on to me. I ran home holding the snake with one hand, and Mr. Snake firmly clamped to my other one. I felt like we somehow needed each other.

I got him home and started to cuddle with him. Snake became my first friend. Here was something that other people found yucky and scary that I could relate to. I've had snakes as pets ever since. I even built a little zoo for myself in my room and filled it with snakes and hamsters and mice. I learned that I could be myself and be totally OK when I was alone with animals—by myself in nature. In nature, I didn't just survive, I thrived.

Days and Nights at Camp

The most important value that was taught in our household was independence. Roger and Georgette totally believed that you had to take care of yourself because no one else would.

I always worked. No matter what. Often several jobs. My very first job was as a seeing-eye dog replacement for a professor friend of the family, a man I called "Amu," my "uncle." He was between animals, his first having died and his second yet to come. For 25 cents a day, I walked him to and from work.

I had two paper routes and worked at a pet store. I sold pieces of gum at school. I would buy it at the store and make a few pennies profit. I believe in the value of hard work. This work ethic is fundamental to what I teach my kids.

In the winter of '77, the city was shut down from the snow. School was closed. But I still had papers to deliver. I couldn't ride my bike or even drag a wagon, so I threw my paper bags over my 13-year-old shoulders and walked house to house to make sure my customers got their papers. It was my job. You live up to your commitments. You work. Except for the two days when the dispatcher couldn't deliver the papers to me, my customers never had a day without their paper. That Christmas I made several hundred dollars in tips. Hard work pays off. But even if I hadn't made an extra dime, I took pride in my accomplishment. For someone who rarely felt good about himself, that feeling of self-esteem was worth more than the money. That's the feeling I want to give my kids.

From as far back as I can remember, I had asthma. By the time I was eight I was going to the hospital three or four times a week. Mama read a book somewhere that said swimming was good for asthmatic children, so she signed me up, and in no time I was at the YMCA almost every day.

I was pretty good. Not great, but pretty good for a fat little kid. Then Roger and Georgette decided that competitive swimming would be great for both me and my brother. We'd both be stronger. Although he was younger, it didn't take long before Chris was swimming in the same competitions, and very soon he started beating me all the time. Then he started winning state competitions. Chris had a natural athlete's body. I did too; I just packed a whole lot of fat around it.

Chris' swimming successes got him more public praise and definitely got him more parental approval and love. Once again I was "less than" and not deserving of love.

One place where I actually succeeded—doing even better than Chris—was at camp.

At first I went to day camp. Camp Tycony. I was eight. A YMCA camp, Tycony had trails to hike, a pond to fish in, woods to play in. It was perfect for me. All the more so because at least for the first year, Chris didn't come.

Every morning I was so excited, waiting for the big green bus to come and pick me up. There were counselors and other kids on board, and I loved it. I loved everything about it. From the early morning ride through the long day, right up to getting dropped back off home in the late afternoon, I had the time of my life. It was me and nature. I got to be away from home.

But like so many things in my life, what started out great ended up a mess.

In my third year there was this older counselor, Daniel, who was about 28, which was a whole lot older than any of the others. Daniel seemed to be looking out for me, and I thought he was a real buddy. He praised me for all my new skills. I had become a real nature boy; I could even catch fish and snakes barehanded. Daniel was always there to give me the extra pat on the back.

The last night of day camp was a sleepover; the big exciting event that we all looked forward to. We had a cookout and a campfire and got to sleep outside under the stars. Daniel convinced me to put my sleeping bag next to his, which was about 50 feet away from the rest of the camp. He said that way we could catch snakes after everyone else had gone to sleep.

He got into my sleeping bag with me and whispered about catching special snakes. He managed to get me naked. I totally freaked out. I was terrified. I didn't know what would be worse—to keep going or to make a scene and be caught.

After Daniel had done what he wanted to do, and while I was still naked, I somehow managed to quietly slip away. I found a pair of pants and a T-shirt to wear. I stayed up the rest of the night staying close to the campfire. Confused, ashamed, and feeling totally betrayed. Someone who I loved had just abused me. Someone who I thought cared about me was only manipulating me to get something. This place that I loved being in was no longer safe, and it certainly stopped being fun. My refuge was violated.

The next morning they held up the lost and found items. All the things that the kids misplaced over the week were shown and claimed. My underpants were brought out. My icky fat boy briefs. Under the best of circumstances I would have been embarrassed to own up to those. On this morning, the sight of them made me nauseated.

When I came home, I started to tell my mother what happened, but stopped, not understanding her reaction, which was silence. By now my humiliation had turned to rage. I wanted to have the guy arrested. Two days went by, and still nothing had been said or done. After a few days I confronted her wanting to know why she was letting this asshole get away with it. She said she didn't know what to do, so she talked to my Uncle Al, the psychiatrist, and he said that as long as I was talking about it, I would be OK. It felt like it was my problem. She said it would be better to let it alone. It was never spoken of again.

I don't know which was worse—being attacked by my counselor or feeling like I had to deal with it alone. It was one horrible situation compounded by another.

Even the Camp Tycony experience could not stop my love of being in nature. Besides, time away from home anywhere was always better. So at age 11, I went off to Camp Tecumseh, a week at a time sleep-a-way. This time with my brother.

The very first week, Chris cried the whole time, which was great. I knew he wouldn't come back. This, of course, made it that much better. I worked out a deal with my dad. He would buy me one week for every one I could pay for. Between the two of us, I managed to secure a whole two months away from home. That made us both pretty happy.

Tecumseh was a Shawnee chief whose name means "shooting star." That's an image I can identify with. A lot of the time I think of myself as the guy who can shine really bright for a little bit, but then I burn up and fall—whether by fate or because of my own self-destructive behavior.

I also identified with the Native American experience. In my mind, they were the guys who were living exactly the kind of life I wanted to live but then someone came in and just screwed them. Their land and culture got raped because of power and greed. There is almost nothing I find as destructive as greed. It's the great poison that kills anything it touches.

A lot of the time I see the world in terms of good guys and bad guys. Too often the bad guys win. That's why I became a mentor. We need to help kids find a way to stand up to the bad guys and survive.

At Camp Tecumseh, I finally became a winner—the expert, the king. From the time I was really little, my dad gave me field guides, and I was expected to know all the various plants and animals. Roger, the geologist, made sure I knew everything there was to know about rocks.

I stayed at Camp Tecumseh for seven summers and worked my way up from camper to counselor. In my third year, I was made a Sagamore. A Sagamore was a great man among the Native Americans who the true chief would look to for wisdom and advice. At camp, it meant that you were chosen and acknowledged as one of the really special kids.

Becoming a Sagamore was my first tribal council. At the final campfire, the new initiates are invited to stay for a secret fire circle after everyone else is dismissed. Then they hold the ritual of the Sagamore Stick. They hand you a big staff carved from one of the trees at camp.

For me, the really big prize followed. Once you have your Sagamore Stick, the counselors—the tribal elders—thank you for being good. Me. Thanked. For being good. For someone so hungry for approval that was like winning a million dollars.

I still have my Sagamore Stick; it's one of my most treasured possessions.

In my fourth year I was made stable boy—a sort of junior counselor. Then in my fifth year, a counselor in training. In my sixth year I became a full counselor.

I finally found the one place where I succeeded by just being me. I was liked by my peers and got approval from the powers that be. I earned it through my hard work and my own skills. It was heaven.

And being me, it wasn't going to last.

I was in my seventh year, and the summer was winding down. One night I was with four other counselors hanging out in the long house. We were getting high just smoking a little weed. We knew it was against the rules, of course, but nobody really thought of grass as anything more than being a little naughty. I'd been smoking pot for several years and had even been caught smoking with my cousin in my aunt's driveway. But this was camp. We were counselors. We were supposed to be the role models.

The camp nurse was going on her inspection rounds. Every night she made sure things were tidy, locked up, buttoned down, and following policy. When we heard her come in the front door, we slipped out the back.

Needless to say, she didn't have to be Sherlock Holmes to figure out what had been going on. She probably smelled it before she even came in. I'm sure it was also easy to figure out who had been involved. While every kid thinks no one can tell when he's stoned, every parent who has seen his kid come home with bloodshot eyes, laughing a little too loudly, and covered with potato chip crumbs, knows exactly what's been going on.

We were rounded up and questioned separately. The others denied it. But I said, "Yeah. Guilty. I'm sorry." It seemed the right thing to do. I didn't want to make things worse by lying.

You would have thought I had confessed to being a serial killer. They went crazy. I was yelled at, kicked out, and sent home with one other guy who also copped to the crime. Two of the kids who held to their stories managed to stay.

By being honest I got smacked. All my sense of self and status was destroyed. Worst of all, Roger got the confirmation that I was a useless piece of crap. Everything returned to normal.

Roger and Me 4

One summer I was promised a dog. I had been begging for one, and to my surprise, they got one—a cute little terrier. But they got the puppy while I was away at camp. My father and brother had time to bond with the little thing before I even got to meet him.

When I got home, Roger said, "Here's your dog. You can name him." My favorite counselor was a guy who sang "Ink-a-dinky-doo" all the time, and everyone called the guy "Inky." I liked him and the name, so I called the dog Inky. Since then I have always had at least one pet named Inky.

Of course Inky had spent all that time with Roger and Chris and was much more their dog than he could ever be mine. It was really bizarre passive-aggressive behavior for them to get a dog for me while I was away at camp.

Not surprisingly, Roger showed Inky a lot more affection than he ever showed me. Chris was the golden boy. Inky was adorable. I was still at the bottom of the food chain.

While I had been buying those sticks of gum on the way to school to earn my extra pennies, Roger bought Chris gum by the case so he could sell it at an even bigger profit.

I needed the money as I was paying extortion to some kids at school who would beat me up all the time. I was an easy target—fat, slow, without skills to fight back, and not enough self-esteem to feel worthy of protecting myself. One day, after being beaten up, I got suspended for bleeding in school. It was classic "blame the victim" stuff. Roger's response was, "You'd better learn how to fight." To tell the truth, I still don't know how. I can be a big, hairy, scary guy and make people think I could kill them, but I really have no idea how to actually fight. Fortunately, I've never had to.

One day, when I was about 14 any pretext of father-son caring ended.

It was a day like any other. I delivered newspapers in the morning. Then I went to swim practice, to school, then swim practice again. Then to work at the pet store. When I came home there was tension in the air. I could always feel when I was in trouble for something the minute I walked through the door. On this day, the hostility level was at high the moment I stepped in the house.

Roger was waiting for me, and he was enraged. I didn't know then what it really was about. Maybe I hadn't locked the door when I left. Maybe one of my teachers told him I was flunking. He and I had lots of fights about education versus vocation. He would taunt me with, "Are you going to work from the neck down or use your mind?" I would snap back that the letters PhD after his name hadn't made him happy.

Whatever it was that he was mad about he didn't even explain. Within a second he just came toward me and raised his arm to hit me. This was a first. No matter how abusive he'd been verbally and emotionally, he never tried to hit me. I grabbed his hand and pinned him to the wall. "Now what are you going to do, old man?" I yelled into his face.

Mama was screaming to let him go. She saw that I had enough anger surging through me that I could potentially kill him. She threatened to call 911. Roger shut her up and practically spat at me, "If you think you're ready to get the hell out of my house, go ahead." I was more than ready, and I stormed out.

From that moment on, Roger and I were pretty much done with each other.

I spent the next couple of nights living in a large concrete storm drain that I had been using as a play fort. During that time, they made no effort to find me. When my rage passed, I knew I had to go home. After all, I was only 14.

When I returned, there was neither greeting nor punishment. In fact nothing was even said. Once again we were back to being four people sharing a house, pretending to be a family.

At 16, I developed a case of pneumonia. Being asthmatic, I was used to having lung problems and feeling like I couldn't breathe. But at swim practice one afternoon I had to stop. I couldn't breathe at all and was told to go home. Naturally, I didn't call for help; I just walked home like I always did.

I must have looked and sounded really awful—bad enough to get Roger to drive me to the emergency room. They diagnosed the pneumonia and discovered that 80 percent of my lung capacity was gone. I was hospitalized for three days. But I got worse. When my lung capacity fell to 90 percent gone, the local hospital in Kokomo determined that the care I needed was beyond their scope and that I should go to Riley Hospital for Children in Indianapolis. They wanted to send me in an ambulance to get me there immediately and were willing to transport me quickly.

Roger said no. I don't even know exactly why. He was a professor at Indiana University, so he must have had insurance. Maybe there was a deductible that he didn't want to pay or something, but he refused and drove the 50 miles with me wheezing on only 10 percent lung capacity.

When we finally got to Riley, I was admitted and had to have my lung tapped. Twice. I stayed for five days. Riley Hospital for Children literally saved my life. I will always be grateful to them.

Talking about my father like this has been really hard for me. I don't want anyone to think of me as some kind of victim. I didn't want to publicly hurt him. I even thought about skipping my whole childhood in my story.

But that would have been a lie. I'm done running from the truth. Roger made up a fantasy history, and it didn't work for him. I am who I am because of everything that has happened to me—good and bad. I try to own all the stuff that's of my own making. But I also have to be willing to stop blaming myself for things I didn't do or stuff that was beyond my control.

I just couldn't be the son that Roger wanted me to be. I'm sure that was a huge disappointment for him. And he couldn't be the daddy I needed. I wish it were otherwise. But that's what it was.

Many of the kids I mentor have fathers who have done truly awful things to them. Some of these kids have been beaten, tortured, and pimped out by fathers who make Roger look like the dad on *Leave It To Beaver*. I tell my kids that they can learn to parent themselves, to become the dad they always wanted. They can learn from their experience what not to do when they have children of their own. Some parents teach by power of example. Some are just lessons of what not to do. Being a good daddy to my own baby girl is one of the most important things in the world to me. I guess I have Roger to thank for that.

One of the things I firmly believe as a mentor is to never give up on someone. No matter what. There is always hope. Maybe Roger and I will come to a better understanding someday. Or maybe not.

Religion was not really a part of our growing up. Science was what was revered. There was a church not too far from the house, and when I was about six, I noticed the manger scene going up before Christmas. Someone told me that the newborn in the little crib was the Baby Jesus. I asked Georgette who the Baby Jesus was. She decided we needed some kind of religious education.

We started going to Sunday school at "The Church With The Baby Jesus In Front." I have no idea what kind of church it was. I'm guessing it was some form of Protestant church. Georgette paid Chris and me a nickel to go to class each week.

It didn't really work out. The rest of the kids had parents who believed in religion, and church was a real part of their lives.

Georgette and Roger were not about to embrace God and take us to worship services. Once again I felt like the outsider. I didn't fit in here at all. Although my house didn't feel like the best place to be, at six it still held the comfort of being familiar, and this was just forced separation. After about six weeks, Sunday school wasn't even worth a nickel to me, and the experiment in religious training was over.

I think Georgette realized that we needed some kind of spiritual discipline. Someone told her that transcendental meditation would be a good thing for me as an asthmatic child. There were enough scientific studies around to show that it had physical benefits. Georgette and I started going to transcendental meditation meetings.

They were held in someone's house, and there were about eight to ten people in our class. The whole mood was very calming, and I thought it all seemed very cool. I loved the idea that I could strengthen my mind enough to conquer anything. People talked about this thing called "cosmic consciousness" and that just sounded like something I wanted to have.

They gave me a "walking mantra." At age 12, I was too young to be able to sit still for a full 20 minutes and focus on a single mantra. A walking mantra is something you can chant while going about your day. I practiced while walking to and from school, while I was delivering papers, or whenever I could. I liked it so much that I tried to convince them that I could handle the more grown-up discipline.

I couldn't. I would just fall asleep. But I kept at it nonetheless. Even if all it did was get me into a deep and comfortable sleep, the escape was worth the effort. After six months of regular meetings, I was ready to be given my own "official" mantra.

It's a beautiful ceremony. You come with an offering. I brought two weeks worth of paper-route money and a bouquet of sunflowers. I got a lot of comments for the sunflowers. It seems no one else had ever brought those. Any time I got approval became a memory that stays with me, and I love sunflowers to this day.

I still practice TM using the same mantra that was given to me that night. When my mind is racing and scattered, meditation centers and calms me. When I can't sleep, I can meditate and then fall asleep.

Georgette and I continued with meetings for about a year, and then it seemed like both of us had gotten what we needed out of regular attendance. I think Georgette grew to like the fellowship. TM had expanded her consciousness enough to recognize the value of some form of spiritual life.

I was searching for something, too. Whether it was spiritual or just a place to fit in, I was on a path. At 14, we came to the Unitarian Universalist Church.

This was a match made in—well, as close to heaven as anything Georgette could ever acknowledge. No dogma. No commandments. There were other scientists in the group who thought that the search for knowledge was the most important.

They met in an old carriage house that I thought was really beautiful. There were people of all ages. They all seemed to me like people who probably didn't really fit in anywhere else. My kind of people. They didn't judge. They just made me feel comfortable.

Best of all, Chris hated it. The lack of structure and rules just made him way too uncomfortable, so he stopped going right away. The Unitarian Church became a place that Georgette and I shared together.

The greeter at the church was a sweet older lady about 5 feet tall named Jenny. From the moment we arrived, she made us feel welcome and comfortable. Her husband, Lloyd, a big, tough-looking man with gray hair, stood off a bit, hanging in a corner. He wasn't scary or anything, but I sensed he was a man of great power. As I watched them, I thought they looked so happy—being themselves and being with each other.

At our second visit, Jenny came up to me with her gentle, loving manner and started a conversation. Very soon, Jenny, Lloyd, Georgette, and me became friends. They started having us over to their farm after church. They owned 100 acres just outside of town. Close enough that I could ride my bike there. Far enough that it was like going away.

They had no children. Georgette needed friends, and she knew that I needed some kind of a male role model. Before too long, Jenny and Lloyd became her surrogate parents and therefore my "adopted" grandparents.

Lloyd was a neat guy. He had been a conscientious objector in World War II and worked for the Red Cross. He did his duty but saved lives instead of taking them. He very much believed that you did things just because they were the right things to do.

He was trained as a chemist—I'm sure that added to the connection he and Georgette felt for each other. He made his money in the perfume business in Indianapolis. I remember looking at impressive pictures of Lloyd in his lab coat mixing things in beakers. At age 60, he came back to the Kokomo area and bought the family farm.

They grew mostly soybeans and corn, rotating the crops every year. That's what you do to keep the soil balanced with the right nutrients and acid ratio. Best of all, at least as far as I was concerned, there were acres of an old apple orchard that wasn't really producing crops but was perfect to build forts and hide out in.

I offered to help them on the farm if they would let me camp out in the woods. Being older, they needed a good hand, and I was always willing to work hard. Deep in their woods, I built my own little camp with a fire circle. I would find a low area and dig a hole. I always felt secure in a hole in the earth, the same way that animals hide. I could build a small fire and no one could see it past 20 feet at the most. No one could find me there. Except Jenny. She somehow figured it out and brought me little bottles of Coca-Cola. But she never betrayed the secret location.

Once again, I found a place to be me. Alone and in nature. It felt like that was the way it was supposed to be.

I honored my work commitment. I loved working with them, and the three of us put in long hours. I was expected to know what to do, and I tried to make sure that I learned how to do it.

Being dyslexic I never learned anything by reading, so I developed every other learning skill. I would watch and listen very carefully. Sometimes I could just guess well. One way or another I could fake it or make you believe I knew what I was doing. Usually.

One time Lloyd and I were pulling up a tree stump using a tractor. My job was to jump up on the moving tractor and stop it. I thought it seemed easy enough. I'd seen it done on TV.

Per the plan, the stump gets yanked, then I run alongside the tractor and jump on. I quickly discover I have no idea how to make the damn thing stop. It's picking up speed and Lloyd—this 70-year-old man—is chasing me down.

I hit something. The tractor crashes. Lloyd's charging at me, and I figure I'm done for. Instead, he checks to see if I'm OK, and then he breaks out laughing. For years I faced anger, guilt, fear, and yelling for breaking even the littlest rule. Here I screw up big time, and he didn't yell at me. He laughed. I laughed with him.

What an amazing lesson! Lloyd taught me that mistakes are better handled through laughter and love. Whenever I'm about to explode in a rage and I don't, it's Lloyd's heart keeping me in line. He showed me the real power of love, and his spirit continues to inspire me.

One would think that my parents would have caught on to my learning disability. After all, they were teachers, and I was a lousy student. When I was about six, they noticed I had a speech defect, and they got me into therapy for my thick "s." To treat my asthma, they got me involved in swimming. But neither one ever questioned my lack of reading skills. It was assumed I was lazy, stubborn, and just not applying myself.

My response, instead of asking for help, was to buy into it. Or to make excuses to myself. I would tell myself that I didn't read because I just didn't like it. Deep inside I believed the message that Roger's disgust communicated: I'm a worthless piece of shit who will never amount to anything.

I couldn't wait to finish school and get the hell out of their house and away from Kokomo.

On January 15, 1982, I graduated from high school. In spite of my shitty grades, I still finished up early. Roger comes home and tells me to get in the car. He actually seems in a good mood. I'm thinking, "Am I actually getting a graduation present?"

We pull up to the bank. Inside, we sit in the president's office and have a happy conversation. Roger signs some documents. He has me sign some others. Then he hands me the keys to the car and tells me it's mine. This five-door Chevy Chevette would not have been my choice, but I thought, "Hey, it's a car. My father just gave me a car!" It seemed too good to be true.

It was. After Roger hands me the keys, the bank president hands me a payment book. I owe $1,100. Roger had just sold me his old piece of crap Chevette at book value and saddled me with debt.

Roger bought himself a new car.

On January 27 I turned 18.

On January 28 I moved out of the house.

Abilene

5

While I was still in high school, I was delivering pizzas at night. Not only did it give me some spending money, it also allowed me to keep out of the house till about 4:00 a.m. I basically came home, slept for a bit, and left for school. By the time I officially moved out, I really wasn't living there much at all.

I used to go to the same Standard Oil station to fill up the delivery car. The night attendant was a skinny, little guy named Don. Although he was at least 10 years older than me, we were mentally about the same age. He was an easy guy to hang out with. Don was a little dirty, a back-woodsy sort of guy, in many ways an outsider—something I always identified with. Some nights I wouldn't make it home, and I just crashed on his couch. Everything about Don was pretty laid back—an easy buddy with a place that was easy to move into. Don's shotgun apartment was my first stop living on my own.

After a couple of months at Don's, I found my own apartment. Four hundred square feet on Mulberry Street in downtown Kokomo. My $145.00 rent included utilities and a Murphy bed. I loved it. I knew it was just a temporary place. My goal was to get out of Kokomo, and I had been looking at other towns. Abilene, Texas, had the lowest unemployment rate in the country at that time. Where many cities of the United States were hovering near double digits, Abilene, an oil-rigging boomtown, was in need of laborers.

At this point I'm earning $3.35 an hour as a pizza delivery boy. The thought of making $8 an hour as an oil rigger starts to sound pretty damn good. Texas A&M had an oil-rigging school that would teach you everything you needed to know to get work on a rig. You had to be 18 to get in. I was finally 18, and I was saving up my money.

One night I get a delivery call to the bad side of town. I always hated those calls since they were usually not real, and even if they were, the tips sucked. But I went. It was a four-plex, and the apartment was on the second floor. I walked up. Rang the bell. No answer. Just as I expected. A bum call. I'm heading down the steps, and as I reach the landing, a voice yells, "Freeze!"

I see a guy with a long barrel gun. That's about all I can see because the asshole has a paper bag over his head with the eyes cut out. He takes my money and my wallet and runs off.

I go back to the pizza place and call the police. They investigate, but of course, nothing is found. The robbery does make the paper, and my assailant is dubbed, "The Unknown Thief." At that time, there was a popular comic on TV whose gimmick was to perform with a paper bag on his head. He was known as, "The Unknown Comic." My being held up at gunpoint is turning into a public joke.

Soon after, I've got some guys hanging out in my living room drinking beers. I was running with an older crowd—guys in their 20s—which at 18 is a real difference. One of these dudes says to me, "What kind of idiot gets robbed by a BB gun?"

No one ever said it was a BB gun. I told the police that I had seen a gun "with a long barrel." It could have been a BB gun, I suppose, but at the time, I wasn't looking that closely. I was in a bad neighborhood, and some guy has a gun pointed at me. That was more than enough motivation to give him anything he wanted.

I realize that this guy knows more about the case than I do. I'm wondering what kind of idiot I am to be having assholes in my house who make fun of me, drink my beer, and probably were in on holding me up.

I thought it was just another example of how messed up Kokomo was and how much I need to get the hell out of there.

I knew that Roger really wanted me to go to college. The oil-rigging school was part of Texas A&M. We talk and he gives me the $1,700 tuition money. He's just as happy as I am to see me leave town and go to school for something. He saw value in going to school, any school. I take that money and whatever else I had saved, sell whatever few possessions I have, and pack up the Chevette—which, at this point, I'm still paying for—and head to Texas.

Within two days I'm in Abilene, living in a Travelodge hotel, and enrolled in oil-rigging school.

Abilene was a quiet, little town of around 100,000 people. Flat, filled with small, single-family houses, there was a feeling of going back in time about 20 years. A place that's 20 years behind Kokomo is really small-town mentality.

The school was a six-week course where they taught everything you needed to know about working the fields. But I quickly discovered that it wasn't cool to say you went to school. You looked like a damn carpetbagger who'd come to town to take their jobs.

Realizing I was new in town and could be whoever I wanted to be, I took a page from Roger's book of tricks and invented a history for myself. Being a geologist's son, I had actually seen water-well drilling, and this wasn't all that different. I claimed to have been a scope-up rigger from the time I was a kid, working wells my whole life.

I pulled into Abilene a screwed-up kid whose father had basically paid him to get out of town. Within six weeks, I was a grown man with a fictional past, working job-to-job as a roustabout on the rigs doing every kind of shit job.

My living arrangement suited my condition in life. I find a 15-foot trailer in one of the worst trailer parks in Abilene. Every kind of low life lives there. But it's mine, and it's big enough so that my snake, Bernice, the Burmese python, has her own room.

I make sure to play with Bernice in front of my door all the time. I want the neighbors to see her. When they ask if they can touch her, I say, "Oh no. She's very dangerous." Nobody ever tries to break into a house where there is a 10-foot python running loose inside.

I start hanging out with a crew buddy named Jim, once again, finding myself among guys about 5 to 10 years older than me. Like so many of the roustabouts, Jim's got some muscle and some bad about him. He's also got a beautiful little three-year-old boy named Max who he gets to see regularly. I like Jim, but I really take to Max.

Max's mama comes to pick him up when I'm over at Jim's. Laureen is a tough Texas girl, gangly, spindly, and with a little snaggle tooth. But I thought she was really pretty in her own way.

As young as 19, I found myself attracted to older women with kids. I liked the idea of a ready-made family. I desperately wanted to be part of a real family. I also figure that older single moms are more likely to accept me, if not out of their own loneliness, then because of their desire to find a stand-in dad for their kids.

Well, I get smitten with Laureen, and I'm flattered that she seems to like me. When she shows up at my place two days later, we fall into bed and into a relationship.

Not too long after, my lease runs out on the trailer, and I find a run-down house in a poor neighborhood for $300. The paint is chipped. Some of the floors are still concrete with nothing over them, but it has two bedrooms. Max can have his own room. We move in. I've got a home, a woman, and a kid. I'm in heaven.

Like so many things in my life, things start going well and I'm sure it's all going to work out, then something goes wrong.

Jim starts showing up. I think it's pretty normal—that he's come by to see his kid. But he starts to time his visits just about when I'm leaving for my night-crew job. I still think nothing of it. Denial is so easy to fall into.

Laureen, Max, and me feel like a family. We spent my first Christmas Eve in Texas together. After we put all the presents under the tree, I went off to work filled with holiday cheer. When I came home Christmas morning, Laureen had taken Max, all the presents, even most of my own stuff, and gone back to Jim.

One very precious gift was left behind. A note from Max. It said "I♥U." Scrawled in a childish hand that was Laureen's but looked like it might as well have been Max's was added, "Thank you for being a good Dad."

Laureen got her ex back for Xmas. I got the axe.

Abilene may have been a boomtown before I got there, but by the time I started working, the boom was going bust. Maybe I had been too eager to get away, so I never really did my homework. Maybe I just had bad judgment. Maybe I was just dealt another bad hand. But before too long the jobs just weren't coming, and I couldn't pay the rent. Within a couple of months, I found myself homeless, living with my snakes in my car under a bridge.

It wasn't all bad. I climbed trees to raid nests, so I could feed my snakes. The weather wasn't terrible. Unemployment was soaring, and there were a whole lot of people just like me. Most of them were OK guys—just down on their luck. Sitting in the park, I bummed a smoke off one guy. We get to chatting, and he told me that I could make money selling my blood.

It's so weird now to look back and see myself homeless and penniless, but there I was. I showed up to the blood bank not having had a meal for a couple of days. When they pricked my finger to get my blood type, I passed out.

They were very kind. Needless to say, they were used to dealing with a population of bums. The doctor gave me $5 to get a Church's Chicken Value Pak and told me to come back. I can still remember how grateful I was and how good the meal tasted. You can be damn sure that I went back.

The deal was that they would take two pints of blood, spin it in a centrifuge, and then give you back your red cells. You get paid $20 and some juice. It takes a few days to recover and be ready to go again, so the most you can go is twice a week. But that was $40 more than I had.

With my first blood money, I was able to buy a gallon jug of gas to keep in the trunk, my own form of insurance.

The Ninja Nurse 6

It was just enough to get me back on my feet. From there I started picking up some extra work as a day laborer, working construction sites doing caulking and wall prep. I really had to get a place to live. The great motivator for me was finding a clean place to take a dump. It never occurred to me to find a men's shelter or any kind of public assistance. I was capable of working, and it was my responsibility to take care of myself.

One day at the blood bank, I meet James who looks pretty good in comparison to the rest of us. He had this clean helmet of hair. James was an apple-picker from Washington State who had also gone to the Texas A&M rigging school and was also out of work. My fellow Aggie alum was living alone in a 2,300 square-foot, three-bedroom, one-and-a-half-bath house. It's totally empty. Totally. Not a stick of furniture. But he tells me I'm welcome to join him.

It was a roof over my head—and a toilet. Things were looking up.

One morning James disappears. No note. Nothing. James seemed to be one who never needed much stuff or many words. Taking it one day at a time, I figure I'll stay and see what happens. When the landlord shows up, I tell him that James is gone and that I would like to take over the house, but I really can't afford it. We make a deal that I will do day labor for him in lieu of rent. Things were definitely looking up.

The largest employer in the area was the Abilene State School, a huge public institution that housed the severely mentally handicapped and mentally challenged. I heard they were hiring, and I really wanted a regular job, so I applied. My landlord let me use his number as a contact.

One day on the job, my boss tells me that the Abilene State School called and wants to see me—now.

I didn't have gas money to make it to the interview so I walked the three miles. Although I was late, my effort supported my pitch—I wasn't just another out-of-work, oilfield guy looking for a fill-in job. I convinced them that I really wanted the job and would do anything.

Two days later, I got hired as a nurse's aide. It's $200 a week which means I can afford rent, food, and even a little furniture to start building a home for myself. I get assigned the 10:00 p.m. to 6:00 a.m. shift on Dorm 46, "The Quiet Dorm."

This unit held about 45 clients who slept in these big open bays. The residents were people of all ages but with the mental age of anywhere from six months to three years. They pretty much stayed diapered and in bed.

My job was pretty easy. I sat in the hallway and listened to them sleep. Periodically, I made rounds and changed the diapers on anyone who was soiled.

The nurse who ran the shift was Bette, a wrinkled, older woman who had been at Abilene State School for 40 years. She wore a blonde, beehive wig and drew her eyebrows on. In my constant search to create family, I latched on to her, and within two months she became my Abilene mom, driving me to and from work and feeding me.

As soon as things are on the upswing and my self-esteem rises from less than none to at least zero, I want to be in a relationship. Being a slow learner at some things, or maybe just stubborn, I ignore the lesson of Laureen and start looking for another older woman with kids.

The supervisor on the shift before me was a dark-haired, dark-eyed woman with a big butt named Gail. She's 10 years older than me and has two little kids, a beautiful three-year-old boy, Jim Bob, who they call JB and who really needs a dad, and Starletta, an eight-year-old girl with an innocent soul and some damage already done to her. Starletta's daddy wanted boys and made it clear to her that she was and would always be inferior—in the world and in his eyes. When I met her, she was clutching her dollies very protectively. I asked her why she held them that way and she told me, "They need it."

I figure that's the kind of kid who needs me and that's the kind of family that I need. I find out Gail has no ex to worry about. Whoever it was, the guy is long gone and there are no fond memories. Gail and I start dating, sleeping together, and very soon I move in with her.

Life in my new home is really fun. I go reptile hunting in the backyard. I take the kids fishing. Now that I have a roof over my head, I can enjoy being outdoors again. When you don't have a choice, outdoors is an unfriendly place, but when it's recreation time, there's nothing like being in nature.

The job is going pretty smoothly. It's easy work. Too easy, in fact. With so little to do, I end up falling asleep on duty. True to form, I get caught. Twice. After being on the job for a year, the supervising night nurse, Charlene, catches me for the third time. She writes me up, and I'm called into HR. The same guy who hired me gives me an ultimatum. Either I take the 2:00 p.m. to 10:00 p.m. shift on Dorm 44 or I'm out.

It's really no choice at all, even though the assignment is the one that no one wants. Dorm 44 is called "The Death Dorm." It's the last stop for the residents of the Abilene State School. And it's my last chance.

When I walk into Dorm 44 for the first time, the stench of death assaults me. There are 50 terminal patients. These are the saddest of the sad. They are not only profoundly disabled; many of them have cerebral palsy, muscular dystrophy, or other severe physical disabilities. Their bodies are rotting away with cancer and bedsores.

These are truly the forgotten ones. Maybe they had a caregiver at one time. Maybe that person died. Maybe that caregiver gave up. But there were hardly any visitors. Almost anyone from the outside world and even the staff just hated the place. It's a room full of totally helpless, incredibly needy, terminally-ill patients. For someone like me who craves to be needed, it's actually a perfect match.

Around this time I turn 20. As I look back, I see that in my efforts to look like a grown-up with a past, I was doing a whole lot of grown-up living but without any of the real maturity to quite understand it all or make it work.

One day, I get a call from Lloyd. He and Jenny are really getting old and having a hard time managing the farm. They ask me to come back and help. So I go back to Kokomo to see them and talk about how this might work. I bring Gail, JB, and Starletta with me.

Lloyd tells me that if I plan to live on the farm with all of them I have to be married. Nothing definite is decided on this trip. We agree to all think about it, and we go back to Abilene. But Gail has had the seeds of marriage sown and is doing some thinking of her own.

One day I call the school and ask to speak to Gail. The girl on the phone says, "You mean Gail Boneham?" I think, oh, Gail's just trying to make it look like we're married. When I get her on the phone, I ask her what the deal is. She tells me that as long as we're planning to get married anyhow, she figured she would just start using my name. That made sense.

Decisions about marriage and moving don't need to be made. Lloyd calls and tells me they have sold the farm and moved into a little house. When I tell Gail, she seems to take it in stride. I think things are just going to continue as they've been. But before too long, Gail starts staying out after work. Then she starts staying out even later. After one night of staying out all night, she comes home and shows me a new car that a "friend" just gave her as a gift.

I may be naïve sometimes. I may jump into deep denial when I don't want to look at something. But I know for damn sure

there's only one way Gail got a new car out of a man friend—
and that's by being real friendly.

I storm out of the house with my prized possessions in tow,
and crash at a buddy's for two days. When I calm down, I
return and the house is completely cleaned out. Everything—
her stuff, my stuff, the kids stuff—all gone. All that's left is
our waterbed. And there's a hose attached to that with the
water draining out.

I was to be the next thing drained dry. I get served with divorce papers. It turns out that Gail was not just using my name
for show or to make the future easier. She had registered us as
a common law marriage. In Texas, six months of living together, a joint bank account, and a document—like a utility
bill—with both our names on it was all she needed to officially and legally become Mrs. Rupert Boneham.

Our only asset was a Chevy Bronco. (The Chevette had blown
up on the street one day.) The court made me sell the Bronco
and give her half. It also made me give her half of our joint
account. That was my life savings; she had never put a dime
into it. She got $4,000.

The money stuff just pissed me off. What made me sad was
losing the kids. Just like Max, I never saw JB or Starletta
again.

I focused on my work at the State School. I busted my ass to
make things better for these people I now considered "my"
patients. I was usually assigned 10 of them. I made sure each
one was clean. If they were able, I got them dressed and up
for part of the day. And those who were up to it, I took outside for a breath of fresh air. I am totally committed to each
one of them, and my superiors start to notice me.

There aren't a whole lot of promotions an aide can get. I can do the work of an LPN, but if I really want to get ahead, I need the right letters after my name. In this case, the letters are "RN," so I enroll in nursing school at Cisco Junior College.

Knowing I have a problem with reading, I don't bother buying books. Instead I listen very intently and tape every class. Cisco is a 50-mile ride. I listen to my classes on the way home and then again on the way back to school.

It works. In anatomy class, I could put my hand in a bag and name the bone blind. By feel I could tell if it was a carpal, a tarsal, or a metatarsal. After all, I had been raised in a house where science was everything. I could make my mind work this way. I managed to get a 3.2 grade point average.

Maintaining grades and work took a whole lot of energy. It was at this time that I got introduced to chemical assistance. I started eating a little speed on the weekends. It was a pick-me-up. At that time and in that world, it was not only condoned, it was also expected. But it opened a door. Later I would not only walk into the room, I'd move into the house.

In the meantime, I get yet another place to live. A two-bedroom house on 18th Street. That gives me a bedroom and another one for my snakes. And before too long, another lady, Sherry Dickson, moves in.

Sherry is young, sweet, cute, and doesn't have kids. I really am trying to change my patterns. I'm holding down a full-time job, going to school, and living with a woman who is age appropriate and seems to really care about me.

The nursing program was structured so that you took your basic science and prep classes at Cisco for two years then trans-

In Texas, when my only means of transportation was the motorcycle, with an old friend.

ferred to San Angelos University, 98 miles away in San Angelo, Texas. To save on gas, I get a motorcycle. For $8, I can drive the Kawasaki Ninja Nighthawk for a week.

Working these 21-hour days took more than a tank of gas and a motorcycle to get through. The little occasional tabs of speed just weren't enough anymore, so I took to snorting it. And when that doesn't work, I start shooting it. I think that I'm OK because I'm not sharing needles. I'm a nursing student. I know what I'm doing. I think I'm handling it. But once again, it's just denial. My life is spiraling out of control. Drugs are just the symptom. Or a futile attempt to run faster than the downward spiral.

But Sherry saw it. She loved me enough that she couldn't bear watching what I was doing to myself. So she left me.

Her leaving me makes me see the tombstones in my eyes. I do what every druggie does when confronted with the problem in such a direct way. I decide to stop shooting. I figure it's the needle not the drug that's killing me. It's such a classic addict's response. It's a load of crap, of course, but at the time it makes perfect sense.

I think that having gone through this—and come out on the other side—I can relate to the kids I mentor in a more real way. I see through their bullshit because I used to sling it myself. And they know I'm talking true because I've been there.

I find a woman who will put up with my shit—a 6-foot-tall, 130-pound, long-haired blonde named Diana who is probably using as much as I am, but I don't see it. And I don't care. I've got another woman and another kid. Diana has four kids, but only one, a little 6-year-old girl, Tracey, is with her. And now they're both with me. And we're all living in a crazy world that's doomed to destruction.

One day, I'm in my surgical nursing class watching a gall bladder operation. The classic profile of a gall bladder patient is female, 40, and fat. And this patient is classic. The surgeon is making all kinds of disgusting jokes about her and really treating her like a big old carcass that needs butchering. All my identification as someone who has felt fat his whole life is with her, and I go into a rage. I storm out of the operating room and decide that I am quitting nursing school that day. Two classes short of my degree and I'm out of there. My thinking is just totally screwed up.

I get on my Ninja and head to work driving way too fast. I'm going 60 to 80 where I should have been doing 35. I am out of control in every way—my life, my thinking, and my driving. I am literally headed for a crash.

With my buddy in Abilene, Texas, just before I moved back to Indianapolis in 1989.

It comes as I career around a bend and hit the rail. I slam into it and get thrown over the bike and land on someone's front lawn. I don't know how long I was unconscious, but when I come to I am lying there thinking about all the people who are passing me without helping me. I think that it's not just me, but this whole town is just messed up. I know that I have to change or die.

I also know that I have to get to work. I pick myself up and check the Ninja to see that it's still drivable. I take myself on to the Abilene State School and see the house doc. He asks me if I was the guy he saw lying there when he was driving to work. I think, "How screwed is that?" Even the doctors in this town don't stop for an accident victim. I could have been dying, and he just drove on.

He sends me to the school infirmary, then they send me on to the ER. I've broken my neck. They give me a collar and some pain pills, and I'm on my way home.

Truck and trailer for the move from Abilene to Indianapolis. The trailer was a boat trailer before I started.

Lying in bed it becomes totally clear that I have to just get away from Abilene, work, school, everything. But I'm not sure what to do or where to go.

Once again fate or God or the Universe or Whatever steps in. Lloyd calls. He and Jenny have become too ill to stay where they are. The little house they bought after they sold the farm was actually in a retirement village. The next stop

The last house in Abilene, Texas, that I lived in.

Me, Lloyd, and Jenny in front of the retirement village they moved to after selling the farm (1985).

would be a nursing home, and he desperately does not want to make that move. I tell him, "I'll be there."

I cash in all my sick days, vacation days, and retirement money from the State School. I'd been there since 1983, and it's now 1990, and I hadn't used up anything. I get about $6,700. That's a whole lot more than I arrived with.

I tell Diana and Tracey that I have to go take care of my adopted grandparents. They want to come. That's just impossible. Knowing full well that I am lying, I tell them that I will come back for them after Jenny and Lloyd die. I think they know, too, but we all pretend it's the truth.

Over the years I had acquired a 1945 16-foot wooden boat. I dragged it into the yard and added a few old steering wheels and left it as a gift to Tracey and the kids in the neighborhood. That was my legacy to Abilene: a rotting, old vessel in a makeshift playground.

I turn the boat's trailer into a flatbed and pack my stuff on it. It takes me two trips to get everything.

When I get back from Indianapolis for the final load, Diana has neatly boxed up the remainder of my possessions. Having been ripped off by Laureen and Gail, it broke my heart to see how supportive she was being in the face of being abandoned by someone she loved. But I had to go.

With tears in my eyes I left, leaving behind a life of drugs and self-abuse, but also leaving my dying patients, a woman who cared, and a little girl who needed me.

Lloyd and Jenny 7

It's May 1990 when I return to Indianapolis believing that I'm doing the right thing coming to help Jenny and Lloyd. I'm hoping that this geographic shift will change my life for the better. Unfortunately, wherever you go—there you are.

All the time I was in Abilene, Georgette had remained close to Jenny and Lloyd. She helped them move from the farm to the retirement village. Knowing I was coming home to help, she bought a two-story house. The plan was for her to live on the top floor, Jenny and Lloyd would live on the first floor, and I would live in the basement and be the caretaker.

Georgette had other responsibilities. After my brother finished college, she and Roger got a divorce. She went back to school in Indianapolis to get another advanced degree. This time in social work. This house in the section of town called

Broad Ripple, the artsy-fartsy bohemian neighborhood, seemed like a perfect solution to everyone's needs.

While I knew I was coming to help my adopted grandparents, I hadn't counted on everything already being in place and a done deal. I felt like I really had no choice but to go along with it. I took most of the money I had and refurbished the basement into my own apartment. It's a dark retreat just like the next turn my life takes.

Jenny and Lloyd require full-time help. His body is just wearing out, and her mind is fading fast. On my first day back, Lloyd drives us to a Steak 'n Shake for lunch. Driving is still the sign of independence that he wants to hold onto, but he's long past the time when he should be behind the wheel. He seems really uncomfortable while he's driving, which I attribute to age. But when we arrive, I discover that the discomfort came from him soiling himself. He's feeling humiliated. I try to comfort him and tell him it's OK, but we're both feeling sad and embarrassed for each other. I put my skills from the State School into play on that very first day and helped Lloyd to the restroom and cleaned him up. I could tell from my experience he wasn't long for this world. He was hanging on to outlive Jenny knowing she would be at a total loss without him. I was going to try to help them both as best I could.

I spend my days taking care of them and the house. At first, I spend my nights retreating to my basement and watching TV. I start staying up all night staring at the screen. I try and keep in touch with the State School since I still care about the patients I had been helping. I'm starting to hear that one by one they are dying. I feel like I failed them. I begin to slide into a deep depression.

I take to wandering the streets at night and hanging out in dingy bars off the beaten track. Even in this nice neighborhood, I could find the seedy places. All around Broad Ripple are upscale clubs where nice people go to socialize and have a cocktail. I find the bars where not so nice people go to get drunk. And I join them.

My hangout is a working class joint located down a dark alley appropriately called the Alley Cat Lounge. It's a real boozer bar with its share of lowlifes who often break into fights. I feel right at home.

Although I am being "paid" for my services at the house, $50 a week just doesn't cut it. I need to get a job. One night I'm drinking away at the Alley Cat Lounge, and the bouncer accidentally hit his head at the service bar and passed out. I got his job.

The great thing about working at a bar—or at least a dive bar—is that you not only get all you can eat but also all you can drink for free. I've sworn off drugs, but in the midst of my depression, alcohol didn't seem like a drug. I start putting away a bottle of tequila and a case of beer every day. I'm staying drunk 'round the clock. Like all drunks, I convince myself that as long as I'm holding down a job, I'm OK.

But even I don't really believe it. I'm sinking deeper and deeper. I feel like I made the wrong decision. I should have stayed with Diana and Tracey and finished school. I should have stayed with the patients. I've messed up big time.

Alcohol and depression feed on each other. And they both lie to you. I could tell myself I was handling everything while at the same time feeling suicidal. The truth is told in the faces of the people who care about you. The bar people don't care.

They ask me to not start drinking until after midnight, not because they are concerned for my well-being, I'm just getting too expensive.

We make it through Thanksgiving. Shortly after that Lloyd goes to the hospital and is put on dialysis. I see the truth in Lloyd's eyes. He knows he's dying, and he knows that I am too messed up to take care of Jenny. He died that night. I took his ashes back to the farm and spread them in the field wishing that Lloyd's last image of me was anything other than the drunk he saw—and mirrored back to me. I hope he has forgiven me. I don't know that I've ever really forgiven myself.

Being a depressed drunk, this just gives me one more thing to beat myself up over. One more reason that proves I'm the useless piece of shit that my parents always convinced me I was.

Lloyd's fears proved true. Jenny completely lost it after he was gone. At 82 she slips back to being a little kid who doesn't know what is going on. I'm pretty useless, and Georgette doesn't have the skills or time to take care of her. They are fighting all the time. I can still picture Georgette wagging her finger in this crazy old lady's face. Neither one knowing what to make of the other.

In the middle of this insanity, Georgette kicks me out of the house. Maybe she can't stand seeing me in a drunken oblivion. Regardless of the reason, I'm out of there. It's back to couch surfing. Georgette is cleaning house getting rid of everyone. She calls Jenny's sister in Chicago and tells her that she has to come and get her.

When the sister comes to cart Jenny off, we tell her that we'll visit and all the other lies you tell a person when the truth is too hard to face. Of course, I never go visit. I never see Jenny again. Within nine months, she's dead.

I collect her ashes and take them to the farm. As I spread them over Lloyd's, I tell her how sorry I am. They'd showed me nothing but kindness, and I failed them. The only thing I managed to do right for them was to unite their remains in the earth that they loved.

Knowing that being homeless sucks big time, I know what I need to do. I move in with the woman I had just started seeing.

Randi Wright was one of the first people I met at the Alley Cat Lounge. A tough, rough-edged woman who works in real estate, she immediately took to me. I only date women who ask me out first; I would never have the self-confidence to ask a woman out. Randi was exactly the kind of woman I latched onto: not the best looking and single with kids.

She owns a four- or five-bedroom house in the Broad Ripple area, close to the bar. Her place is filled with misfits and drifters as she rents out the extra rooms to musicians, painters, and writers, the kind of people you'd expect to find in this bohemian section of town.

Her 11-year-old daughter, Stacey, is a honey who tries to be good, to do well in school, and to please everyone. Even when I keep calling her "Tracey," she's such a sweetie that she never corrects me.

Randi's older kid, Sam, is 13. He's a tough guy hanging with a bad crowd—and he's the leader. He already runs a chop shop for mopeds. Sam and his buds have figured out that if you pull enough shit at school they throw your ass out. For kids who don't want to go to school in the first place, this is the perfect tactic. Once you've been kicked out, no one can discipline you for not going.

Or so Sam thinks.

Because I'm the one who's basically home all day, Randi gets behind my handling Sam. I tell him, "OK, if you're not going to school, you're going to work." I start taking him and his gang around the neighborhood doing odd jobs: trash removal, simple rehab work, any kind of day labor stuff that will force the kids to do something useful with this "time off."

Some days it does take literal force. I have to grab him and hold him, so he doesn't run away. I'm a big guy and can seem pretty scary, so I never have to do much more than just wrap my big arms around him. Once my immediate threat stops him cold, I can talk softly into his ear and explain why we're doing this. That it really is in his best interest to be useful and not turn into a bum. I can tell him what being a homeless drug addict feels like. My restraint turns into an embrace. Sam becomes the first of "my kids."

Rupert's Kids

8

I often say that Sam and his gang of would-be delinquents were the first of Rupert's Kids to be helped. The truth is, they made me want to be better. Their youth showed me hope. My deep desire to make things better for them brought me back from self-destruction. The first person who was really saved by Rupert's Kids was Rupert.

My years of working in the mental health community started to pay off in a completely different way than I had expected when I signed on to the Abilene State School. There we took care of the hopeless and the abandoned. I knew in my fat gut that here I was working with kids who could be saved. Having felt abandoned, abused, alone, screwed up, drugged out, and desperate for approval, I knew exactly who these kids were, what they were feeling, and the kind of loving discipline they needed. And just like I could see Lloyd's disappointment in his eyes when he saw a drunk, these kids could see in my eyes

71

that I really cared. We could look each other in the eye and know the truth.

I decided to form an organization: Kids Helping Other People Exist. Kids HOPE. I incorporated. But I had no idea how to run a not-for-profit program. I never got my 501(c)(3) status. Fundraising was a mystery. And there were plenty of expenses. On the job, the kids needed to eat. Some of them needed a safe place to stay. One of the key things to making mentoring successful is to demonstrate to each kid that you will never abandon him. No matter what. I know I can make this work even if I can't secure funds. After all, I had plastic. Kids HOPE was basically funded on my credit cards.

Kids started showing up. I reached out to work with the Hamilton County Court System. Indianapolis is in Marion County, but I wasn't established enough to deal with the big city. Hamilton County is the next county out, a more small-town, rural area. It's a lot easier to become more personally involved with a simpler world. They were willing to send me their "walking wounded," the kids who were falling through the cracks and ordered to do community service. I become known as running a place where they will actually do the work, not just someone signing off on their showing up. Kids HOPE is growing from Sam and a few of his gang to about a dozen kids.

I'm being helped a lot by a guy named Hank, a friend of Randi's who also hangs out at the Alley Cat Lounge. Hank's a carpenter, and he's really good at working with the kids and teaching them basic skills.

I realize that being a bouncer in a joint like the Alley Cat isn't the best modeling for my kids, so I start looking for other work. I end up with a part-time gig as a cook at Crackers Comedy Club. It's still a bar, so I can keep boozing, but it's a whole lot classier.

Once again, things seem to be looking up. And once again, the pendulum starts to swing back toward the dark side.

Although Randi is fine with the way I'm helping Sam, she doesn't like the feeling that we're really starting to behave like a family. She's used to being independent and running things her way. All this closeness starts to scare her. So she kicks me out.

I'm determined to stave off what I feel is impending disaster. I find crappy apartments that need work and trade labor for rent. I end up sharing a place with a bud from the Alley Cat named Steve.

Steve has a girlfriend who works at one of the fancy-pants clubs—the Club 816. We end up there many nights after our drinking at work, and we continue to party after we get there. It's not the kind of place we would normally choose to go to, but when it's really late and mostly just the help hanging out, it's OK.

One of the servers there is a cute little blonde with pale skin and blue eyes named Sharon. I think she is totally out of my league, and I am sure that she is never going to be one of the women who come on to me. But she's so adorable I somehow muster up the courage to ask her to lunch. To my total amazement, she accepts.

Lunch goes really well. We seem to get on better than I would ever have expected. Even better, she drinks like me. She likes that I can at least keep up with her. In fact, she may even drink more than me, but when you're drinking that much, who's counting. We have another couple of lunches. We go to dinner and get really wasted, and she comes home with me. When we woke up the next morning, we cracked open a bottle of Cuervo and tossed the cap out the window. We continue our binge, stay in bed, and by the end of the day, we're a couple. A couple of drunks, but a couple.

We decide to move into a place together. We find a four-plex condemned dump with a "for rent" sign out in front.

I meet the landlord who is a typical shady good ol' boy slumlord. We agree that I will do some repairs in exchange for rent. I do some clean up. Fix the toilet. He sees that the place is starting to look OK so he works on adding a basement apartment.

One day I get a $500 electric bill and a disconnect notice. There was no way that the two of us could have possibly used up that kind of power. We were rarely home and if we were, we were drunk or passed out.

It turns out that Mr. Slumlord has been jumping my power cables to feed the basement and every other place in this dump that he is turning into a flophouse. The electric company won't do anything to help me. So I let them shut everything off and Sharon and I just move out.

In my heart I know that disaster has to be around the corner. I'm hoping that if I stay drunk enough, it won't hurt so much when it finally comes.

Right after my 30th birthday, I get the wake-up call. I get pulled over by the cops one night and blow a .27 blood alcohol count, more than double the legal limit. They haul my ass off to jail.

I need $115 to bail my sorry ass out. It might as well have been $115,000. I don't have any money of my own. I've been barely covering my meager expenses and drinking away the rest. I'm up to my ears in plastic debt from helping the kids.

I call home. Steve and Sharon are either too drunk or too broke themselves, so they won't come. To be honest, I don't remember the details. What I do remember is sitting in a cell realizing that at 30 years old I have no money, no real friends, and no future. I've screwed up again. Made all the wrong choices. I can't even use youth and inexperience as an excuse.

I realize I have got to make a plan. A 10-year plan. I decide that in the next year I have to own my own place. Couch surfing and relying on women to take care of me won't work anymore. I need a roof over my head, a toilet to take a dump, and a deed to call it my own. But for now, in this cell, I see myself one more time as a useless piece of shit.

I make the one phone call that I hate making but believe will get me out of this. I call Mama. While my relationship with Georgette has been on again, off again, and rocky at best, I pray that she won't let me down in this real crisis. My prayers are answered. Georgette shows up, bails me out, and takes me back to my place.

I start de-toxing, and I'm a mess. I don't know about rehabs. I don't know that people can have seizures or hallucinations when the booze starts to ooze out. What I start to feel is just awful in every way. I get stomach cramps. My head is pounding. I'm sweating like a pig and sicker than a dog. I try to sleep and drink lots of water. Nothing really helps. It's like having the hangover of a lifetime intensified a thousand times.

I discover that alcohol keeps your feelings at bay. Without that anesthetic, you have to feel shit. The one feeling that I've got coming up is anger. No, rage. I am pissed off at everything and everybody. I'm a mess. The world sucks. Steve and Sharon are useless assholes who couldn't put $115 together to bail me out of jail. They didn't even show up. And even now, they're still drunk around the clock. Steve is paying half the rent, so I have to deal with him. But I throw Sharon's drunken ass out. I have no tolerance for myself or anyone else.

The good news about de-tox is that it finally ends. Life starts to look so much better. As the rage subsides, hope returns. But the memory of how awful it was stays. I remember how screwed up I was before and how truly miserable I was cleaning up. I may drink some now, but the memory of those disgusting, awful, painful days is a big part of what keeps me from ever going back to that level of abuse.

After about five days, I decide it's time to go back to work. I'm not sure if I still have a job. I haven't called in sick. On the other hand, they haven't called me either to find out if I'm OK or to tell me not to bother coming back. To be honest, I don't know. There's a lot of blurry memory there. They might have called or not. Regardless, I just show up for work at the comedy club.

At this point, I am the night manager, and even stone-cold drunk, I was doing my job OK. I guess they figure that sober I'll be dynamite. They put me on 30-day probation, and I'm back in business.

I really start focusing on my long-term plan. My number one task is buying a house. As often happens when I'm in a positive frame of mind, other things start falling into place out of nowhere.

Hank comes by and tells me he needs help working on a duplex he is rehabbing. I never turn down work, so I go with him to look at the place. It's one scary, run-down dump in a really rough neighborhood. One side is a board-up, and the other is a crack house. Hank tells me that the owners want to sell but figure they can't because of the horrible condition this place is in. I figure I can probably buy this thing pretty cheap.

The owners are asking $21,000. Not only that, they only want $1,000 down, and they will hold the mortgage till I pay them off—at $300 a month. As far as I'm concerned, it's a win/win, so we shake on it.

The night before I'm due to sign all the papers, I decide to just hang on the street and see what the neighborhood is like after dark. At around 11:00 I park my old beater pick-up on the street and just watch. I see a party going on two houses down from the place I'm buying. As it gets closer to midnight the traffic increases. Suddenly gunshots go off. People start running from the house. The big picture window is busted.

The weird thing is that no one seems to care. No cops show up. No neighbors come out to see what happened. It's like watching TV. This is what's normal for this neighborhood. I ask myself if this is really what I want to get myself into. For $1,000 down and $300 a month, the answer is—you bet. It will be my own place.

I meet my next-door neighbor, a sweet old man. He tells me he has two dogs who like to sleep on my porch and asks if I would mind if they kept that up. Then I see the dogs. One is a sort of Great Dane-German Shepherd mix; the other is some other kind of big mutt with a lot of St. Bernard in him. These are two monster dogs. They sniff me out. I pet them. I now have my nighttime security system in place ready to go.

The next day I show up with some backup—a couple of cop buddies that I know from the bars. I have the keys, and I let myself in. There are some messed up dudes and a big mess inside. I take the door off its hinges, throw it down, and yell, "It's time for you to go."

One thing I have learned in my years as a hairy-scary man is that if you look like me and act insane, no one will test you. Standing fiercely in an open doorway, I look totally crazy. Not one of them is about to try and see just how nuts I am. It helps that there is a cop car parked in front of the house. They're gone.

Within a week I have the place cleaned out, and I move in. Within two weeks, Hank moves in as a roommate. It only takes another few weeks to furnish the place with found items and stuff from The Salvation Army and Goodwill. I've learned that you can find three broken refrigerators on the street and take them to a shop where they will trade you one working unit for those busted three. You can find all kinds of stuff on the street. What you can't use, you can sell.

My house becomes a place where some of my kids can stay if they need to. I also rent out the extra rooms to college kids and artists who need a place to carry them over. I show the kids how you can live on $18 a week. I teach them how to collect trash and resell it for cash.

I've got myself a roommate, tenants, a place for my snakes, a space for my kids, two scary dogs for protection, and a roof over my head with that toilet I need—and it's mine. Step one—accomplished.

Step two is about finding a way to keep my mentoring program going without totally subsidizing it on my own personal plastic and deepening my debt. Hank and I read about funding being available for community development. So we form the Near North Eastside Community Development Corporation. Neither one of us knows anything about how to do this, but it sounds good and feels promising.

Hank hooks up with some suits who seem to know about grants and funding. We start having a few meetings, and I quickly realize that these guys are coming from a completely different place. For me, it has always been—and always will be—about the kids. That's how I'd gotten so deeply in debt, making sure my kids had something to eat when they were hungry and some shelter and clothing when they needed that. These guys understood business and how to make money. I am not averse to money—making it or having it. But the one emotion I can't stomach is greed. And these guys were greedy.

They start showing us how we can make $1,000 for every $100 that goes into actually serving the kids. I just am trying to keep myself from going deeper in the hole. I sure don't see myself taking money away from the kids. I can't figure out what the suits are doing to deserve much of anything let alone the big bucks.

It becomes clear to me that everything has to change. I am in the midst of changing everything about my life, and this is a big part, so it's got to start clean and clear, too. I dissolve the Near North Eastside Community Development Corporation and Kids HOPE. I keep working with my kids and decide that

I'll figure out how to create something that will somehow fund itself, but it's going to be something new and different.

Meanwhile back at Crackers, I decide that some changes have to be made, too. We can't seem to keep our ushers who make a few bucks an hour doing all the dirty work in addition to seating people. I take out an ad for "Management Trainees in Charge of Public Relations." The "trainees" will still have to usher the patrons, will still be cleaning the bathrooms, and will be making $5.35 an hour, but they will have a title.

Fifteen show up. We hire five of them. They don't last very long. Except for two hard-working winners.

One is Bradley, a great kid just out of accounting school trying to create a future for himself. I figure he can end up doing all kinds of the business work for us down the road.

The other is a girl who already has two jobs. One is in real estate, and the other is clerking at J.C. Penney. This is exactly the kind of person I've been looking for. Someone who actually likes hard work. The fact that she's good looking and a sweetheart doesn't hurt either. Her name is Laura.

Laura

9

Laura Tyner was young, eager, cute, and sweet; she also had a tough side that was no bullshit. She could be all girly and smell pretty, and she could work her ass off cleaning the place up. I was impressed from the start.

Laura had grown up on a farm, so hard work was just part of what you did. She was a good country girl who was comfortable being outside and playing with animals. After graduating from Ball State University in Muncie, Indiana, she moved back to the farm with her folks while she was putting her life together.

Fortunately she came into my life at the right time. I was clean and sober, which was a big plus and a first for me. I'm trying to figure out how to live my life differently, so I'm in no hurry to jump into another relationship. My focus is on cleaning up my act and figuring out who I am, what I want, and how to move forward in a positive way. Although Laura and I get a little flirty with each other, we soon discover that we do really well together as friends.

We seemed to have a lot in common. We liked old cartoons like *Tom & Jerry*. I made a crack about Wally Gator, and she knew who I was talking about. We liked the same kind of rock and roll music although she sometimes had a taste for techno-crap, and I would tease her about that. Laura had even worked in nursing homes as an aide and had gone to nursing school for awhile. She understood about taking care of people.

After about a year of paling around, we unexpectedly end up going on vacation together. I decide to go to Vegas for a Grateful Dead concert. While I was not one of those Dead Heads who spent their lives going around the country following the band, I had been to a lot of concerts and was definitely a fan. In fact I bought my first tie-dyed tank top at a Dead concert in Irving, Texas.

The plan was that Hank, another buddy, and I would go to the concert and spend a week in Vegas playing. It's been forever since I had taken a vacation, and this seemed like a great idea. So I go ahead and pay for the whole deal—three tickets and hotel.

For whatever reason, our third backs out right away. So I ask my friend Laura if she wants to go. I tell her she'll have to pay her own gambling costs, but airfare and hotel are covered. She thinks it'll be a blast. Then Hank gets a little squirrelly about going away with me and her together. He's never really been comfortable around women and certainly not with one as a friend. He's also feeling a little threatened that Laura is taking his place in my life.

I've already paid for everything, so Hank or no Hank, Laura and I decide to go. Being the manager, I give her the time off. With $1,000 in my pocket, we head off for Vegas in time to arrive for the Saturday night show. We discover that Hank still had the concert tickets. We're in too good of a mood to let even that bum us out. We spend Saturday night at the casino and figure we'll go to the Sunday show.

When we get to the Sunday show, of course, it's already sold out. There are some scalpers around, but buying double-priced tickets to a Dead show is just plain wrong. Sell-out or not, I am determined that I am going to see this show and not over-pay for it. I head for the box office as everyone else is walking away disappointed. I hear that they are releasing a few more tickets so I move closer. The security guard tells me that they are all sold out. I point to a guy buying some tickets and tell the guard that I want two. Sure enough, he gets them and sells them to me.

It's a great show. The Dave Matthews Band is the opening act, and everyone is stoked by the time Jerry and the band come on. I am seeing friends that I know from previous concerts. I am having a terrific time, digging the music, feeling part of the crowd, and being with Laura.

The first night I blow $500—half my stake for the week. I've decided to play with a $1,000—win, lose, or draw. The next night, I win two grand. I cash out twenty $100 bills and leave the casino with eighteen of them still in my pocket. It's pouring and I don't care. I'm feeling way too good, and I'm still not drinking anything but coffee and soda.

When I get back to the room, I lay out the bills all over the place so they can dry and so they can surprise Laura when she

The final day of my first date with Laura, getting ready for our helicopter ride over Las Vegas.

wakes up. Naturally she is just giddy when she finally does awaken to a room full of $100 bills. This means we can spend the rest of the week doing anything—it's all covered.

The rest of the week is perfect. Laura and I spend enough time together to enjoy each other's company but not all the time where we might get on each other's nerves. I gamble the nights away; she goes to bed early. When I get up, I join her at the pool, and we eat, play the casino, and do whatever until she gets tired and heads back to the room.

By the end of the week, we're down to $300, and we decide to take a helicopter ride over Vegas as the sun goes down. The tickets are $200, and I tip the guy the last $100. We have a spectacular ride watching all of Vegas light up. It's a magical moment together. We both know that we're not just buddies any more.

Sure enough, for the next year, while we're not officially living together, she's spending a whole lot more time at my place than she is at the farm.

I get to feeling it's time for another vacation. This time it's going to be with some guys—old high school buds that I somehow managed to stay tight with through all these years. Maybe not tight exactly, but close enough where it looked like it would be fun to go camping with them.

Ron, Jack, and his brother DJ, and I pack our gear and take the train to Glacier National Park in Montana where we plan to spend two weeks totally back to nature.

The first week we hike off fairly close to the base camp but still out there on our own. We come back to base to clean up and plan out the second week. We decide to hike 16 miles off any path deep into the park. It's gorgeous. Mama Nature and I are having a perfect reunion. When you're tossed out into the cold with no place to live, outdoors isn't fun, pretty, or inviting. But when you choose to go out and you know there's a place to come home to, there is nothing like Mama Nature to bring you peace of mind and clarity of thought.

One day I go off by myself to go fishing on top of this mountain. The day is perfect. Clean air and blue sky. As I'm fishing, I see an eagle soar by, and he's incredible. I see a light snow gently descending over a waterfall. It's mystical. It's magical. I start to have an out-of-body experience.

In front of my eyes, I see myself. Then I see myself with Laura. It feels right. I see my daughter. I see Laura and me growing old together—like Jenny and Lloyd with all that love. I see that my life will work out. It will all be OK. Me, Laura, and a baby girl. We're going to be fine. I see it all. And I know it is all true. Perfect.

Naturally I don't tell the guys, but when I get home, I tell the one person who has to know. While I don't say I had an out-of-body, mystical vision—I don't want her to think I'm crazy or I got drunk or anything—I just tell Laura, "You're the one." I ask her to move in with me.

I tell Georgette that I want to marry Laura. She couldn't be happier. She gives me her wedding and engagement ring to give to Laura. Georgette and I have always tried to work things through, but neither of us quite knows how to do it. In truth, she always showed up when the chips were really down as long as I came to her and asked for help. Here I came to her with good news, and she made this generous gift. I knew she would. In fact, that's why I went to her with the news before asking Laura. I didn't go because it was the right thing to do or because I wanted her blessing. I went to her because I couldn't afford a ring, I knew she had those rings that she wasn't wearing anymore, and I was pretty sure she would give them to me. I was right. I know it was shameful manipulation, but we both got something we needed. She got to be a loving, generous Mama, and I got the rings.

I have the rings for a couple of months, but I want to find just the right time and place to propose. I take Laura to Kings

Island, an amusement park outside of Cincinnati, Ohio. Laura and I are both roller coaster freaks, and Kings Island has some of the best in the country. Most of my life has been a roller coaster, and it seemed like a great place to ask someone to share the ride with me.

Laura is pretty much on to what's up. We're in the line for the Outer Limits, a big, fast, scary ride, and I'm worried about the rings in my pocket. I must have been fidgeting with them or something because Laura turns to me and says, "Are you ever going to ask me to marry you?"

"Yeah!"

"When?"

"How 'bout now?"

I put the rings on her finger.

We get on the ride.

As we walk down the park play area we see one of those "milk bottle toss" games. It's a carny booth where you throw a ball and try to knock a stack of these metal bottles over and win a prize. The guy behind the counter is wearing a nametag. "Rupert!" I have to talk to him. There are very few of us out there.

After I introduce myself and we share how neat it is to meet another Rupert, I tell him that I just proposed and introduce my fiancée, Laura. Rupert sets the bottles up so that a breeze could knock them down. I throw the ball and win a huge, blue stuffed dolphin.

My life dream is becoming a reality.

We set the date a year away: September 6, 1997. Laura wants to have a big church wedding with all the stops pulled out, and it will take a year to get it all together. That's part of her dream, and I want her dreams to come true. Her agreeing has made my biggest dream a reality. She's really making huge sacrifices to be with me.

Laura's family goes back seven generations in Indianapolis. Acres and acres of what is now the expensive north side of town was originally land farmed by her family. Over the years, some of the land was sold to developers for a great deal of money. On the one hand, Laura is a hardworking farm girl. On the other hand, she is used to having a certain level of creature comforts. She must really love me, because the house we're living in, the $21,000 duplex, is in the heart of the 'hood. It's definitely not the kind of place she was used to. But she is willing to make a go of it with me even in this dump in the ghetto.

After a few days back, I tell Laura the story of my epiphany. I want her to know that I deeply believe that we are meant to be partners and to grow old together. She tells me that she remembers when she first saw me, 10 years earlier at the Alley Cat, she thought, "That's a good one." Everything feels really right for both of us.

I leave out the part about seeing a little girl in my vision. I have abused my body so much that I am convinced I cannot make a baby. I had lived with several women by this point, and none of them had ever gotten pregnant. None of them were really practicing birth control, and I certainly wasn't taking precautions either. So it must be that I just am not capable of fathering a child. I don't want to tell Laura something that can't possibly happen. She might start doubting the rest.

I become determined to make a better life for us. Laura and I both quit the comedy club. She goes to work at a fitness center managing the front desk, and I take on a lot of handyman and rehab work. I had gotten pretty good at it back when I was trading labor for rent. Now I can sell those skills. In addition, I can rescue things from these private jobs and take them to the projects that my kids are working on.

No matter what had been happening in my life, the ups and downs, I managed to have kids around who needed my mentoring. Some would end up living with us, while some just came by and were part of the vocational program. Laura described us as a dysfunctional family who all happened to find each other. And we all took care of each other.

Laura and I buy a cinderblock bunker at a city auction for $300. It's a perfect house for my kids to work on and learn everything about construction. That place needs it all.

I refinance the duplex, so I can pay off the original note, and the house is mine. I already have tenants. Hank is still there plus a musician and another guy as well.

Before too long, I am able to flip the bunker and sell it for $1,500. We buy another house for Laura and me to live in. Laura's parents help finance our new home: an $18,000 shell with no plumbing, no wiring, and no furnace. It's on Guilford Street, not far from the duplex and still in the roughest part of town. But I know that I can turn this into something nice for us. Not luxury for sure, but nice.

In the meantime, I create a fortress of solitude upstairs at the duplex to try and make Laura comfortable in the midst of this battle zone. I build a suite that includes a nice bedroom, a washer and dryer, and a skylight over the bathroom where I install a whirlpool tub. The rest of the house is really rough, and the neighborhood is even rougher, but we've created a little safe haven for ourselves in the middle of it.

Laura's mom, Janet, is not really pleased with any of this. She figures that any white guy living in that neighborhood has to be a bum. For the most part, she's right. I'm sure that I don't look like what she imagined her daughter married to. But she doesn't really make waves, just stays kind of distant.

One Wedding and Many Funerals

10

Her father, Bill, and I get on really well. I like him a lot and start thinking of him as my dad right away. He reminds me of Lloyd in many ways—a good, decent man who loves his family and wants the best for them. If I make Laura happy, he's fine with it.

Bill is on the executive board of the Union Chapel Church where the family has been members for all those many generations. He tells me that the job of cemetery caretaker has opened up, and if I want it, it's mine. It pays $500 a month and includes a house with utilities paid. I take it. Because it's a church-run place, I can't move in with Laura until after we're married. But the plan is to take occupancy right after the honeymoon and get ourselves out of the 'hood.

The job is hard work, but I like it. I always like being outdoors, and there's no place more quiet or more peaceful than

Me and my buddy, Bill, had two graves to dig after a long day at the track. We are in a freshly dug grave at the Union Chapel Cemetery waiting for a pizza to arrive.

a cemetery. I'm working on 27 acres of land with woods and a river. I mow, weed, and when the time comes, dig the graves then fill the holes after the mourners leave. But I'm surrounded by nature, and I know that soon I'll be living here as well.

September 6, 1997, comes and we have our storybook wedding in the Union Chapel Church. About 300 people fill the pews. Laura looks exactly like a perfect bride in her long white dress. I'm in formal wear, too. As out of place as Laura is in the 'hood, that's how out of character I feel in fancy-pants clothes. But I want it all to be exactly the way she's dreamed.

Most of the guests are Laura's friends and family. I really don't have that many true friends in town, but I'm hoping that the wedding will give me an opportunity to make some kind of peace with my family. Georgette is there of course. Roger, who I'd barely seen in 10 years, shows up, but there's no scene of reconciliation. Neither of us have the words or the skills to work that through. But he's there, and I know that for him that's a big thing. Just as he knows that my inviting him is a big step for me.

My brother Christopher was already married, and even though I had been invited to his wedding, I didn't go. I'm sure I made up some kind of excuse, but the truth is that I just wasn't ready to see him happy and successful. He was already working as a pharmaceutical rep in charge of a whole regional team. He's making huge money. Pharmaceutical reps can make a bundle. Chris is a great salesman.

I know that I should have gone. I have so many shoulda-coulda-wouldas, and this is just one more. But I want my niece, Cassidy, to be our flower girl. I really love her, and she kind of reminds me of me. She's got the round Boneham face and, at three, is already running around the woods catching bugs. That's my little flower girl. On some other level, I hope I can make amends with Chris and see if my marriage can start a new chapter.

Chris lets Cassidy be a part of the wedding but tells me that he has to be in Hawaii on business for that day and won't be able to make it. His wife, Lisa, comes with Cassidy and their younger kid, Conner, who's just a baby. I'm grateful for that. I even got to carry Conner throughout the rehearsal dinner. Holding him was a connection to my brother and a buffer from the family all at the same time.

Roger and Georgette paid for the rehearsal dinner. Bill and Janet gave us a week in the Cayman Islands for our honeymoon. It's a really generous gift on top of paying for a wedding that cost more than I sometimes made in a year. I really wanted to take a whole month off, but, of course, I didn't have the money for that.

As the wedding approached, I started planning for how to create my extended honeymoon. I signed up for all those time-share presentations that give you a trip and lodging if you are willing to sit and listen to the spiel. I managed to string a bunch of them together so that we went to Orlando for a few days and listened to a spiel, then a cruise to the Bahamas and another spiel, then a trip to the Keys and still another spiel. I parlayed the thing into the month I wanted.

We ended with a camping trip in Mount Ida, Arkansas, where we went crystal mining. Being a geologist's son, I've learned about rocks, and I think that crystals are one of Mama Nature's miracles. I'm not sure if I believe in all the healing properties that some people claim they have. But when I was trying to stop drinking, I carried around amethyst because the Goddess Amethysta was said to protect drunks, and drinking from an amethyst chalice was supposed to keep you from getting intoxicated.

I usually wear a necklace that's a crystal wrapped in copper wire which acts as a conductor of the stone's energy. The crystal itself channels positive energy focused on me. I do believe that.

At Mount Ida you pay $20 a bucket and can take all the stones you can carry. I carried about 100 pounds in two buckets. I was counting on bringing a whole lot of positive energy into my new marriage.

As soon as we got back to Indy, Laura and I moved into the caretaker's house at the cemetery. My 10-year plan is working out. I have a couple of properties that I own; I'm living in a house in rustic beauty. I have a full-time job, and I have married the woman that I had an epiphany over. The part that was missing was finding a way to make money with my mentoring rather than supporting it with my plastic.

I don't know if it's the crystals, but Georgette shows up with a kid named Rick. She'd been working with Choices, an umbrella that serviced a lot of clients from different organizations. One of them, the Dawn Project, was for last stopper kids in the juvenile court system. These are the kids who are one step away from becoming prisoners instead of juvenile offenders. Rick is a sweet kid—15 years old, 5 foot 2 inches, 120 pounds—but acts like a tough little sucker, doing drugs and being violent with an all-aggressive attitude. He's been kicked out of every other program because whenever someone tried to get him to comply he just beat the shit out of them.

I sit Rick down, talk with him, and explain that I'm his last shot. I am very clear. He can work with me or go to jail. Forty hours a week with me has got to be better than full time in the joint. So he agrees.

We concentrate on the real basics of getting along in the world. You have to go to work. You have to make money or you die. You have to show up, and if you're not the boss, you have to take orders from somebody. You have to do your best. For a kid like Rick, these lessons are huge. They're more important than the skills he's learning working with me at the cemetery. Yes, he's learning how to take the weed-eater apart and put it back together and how to do basic landscaping and mainte-nance, but what he's really learning is the fundamental skill of being responsible. I make sure that he knows that I am count-ing on him to succeed and that I believe he can. I know that at some point he will start to believe it too.

It works. Within six months he's back in school and maintain-ing a schedule.

Georgette gets the Dawn Project to pay me for mentoring. I'm now earning something to do what I love.

Me with Raya and Laura at the Indy 500 parade. (Photo by Jimmy Swan)

After a hard day of work running cables under the Indianapolis Motor Speedway. I am the second from the left.

Here we are at Central Park in New York City during a photo shoot for
People *magazine.*

In a tux, at our wedding reception, cutting the cake with Laura.

Laura and me camping in Kentucky in 2002.

Me at my first stage show in Warsaw, Indiana. (Photo by Jimmy Swan)

Raya and me at our favorite fishing hole on the north side of Indianapolis in 2005.

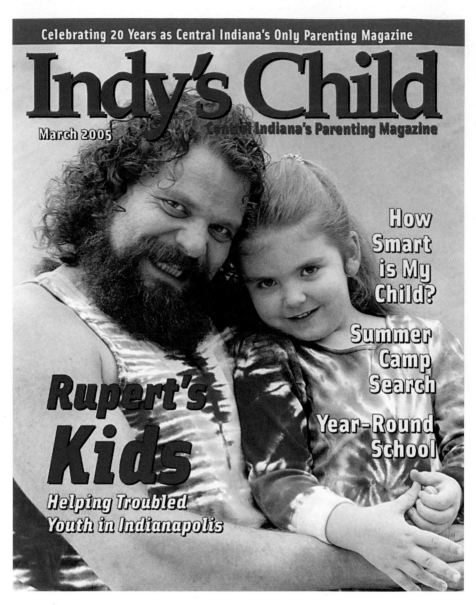

Indy's Child

Central Indiana's Parenting Magazine

March 2005

How Smart is My Child?

Summer Camp Search

Year-Round School

Rupert's Kids

Helping Troubled Youth in Indianapolis

Raya and me on the March 2005 cover of Indy's Child *magazine. (Image provided by* Indy's Child *magazine. Design by Brian Horner. Photo by Scott Barrett)*

Just Being a Dad

11

Out of my hourly rate, I pay Rick so he gets the feeling of earning a paycheck for hard work. I also have to cover all the expenses like lunch and transportation. I tell him exactly what I get, what he gets, and what the rest of the money is for. I want this to be totally transparent and for him to understand how he is not only pulling in money for himself but also actually contributing to the organization as well. And I am still actually making some money working with my kids instead of sinking deeper into debt because they need more than I have. Before too long, I'm up to three kids.

As 1998 begins, our life is settling down, and our relationship is deepening. Laura asks me to stop smoking. I tell her that I will quit when she gets pregnant. I figure it's a safe bet because I am still convinced—in spite of the epiphany—that I

I took this picture of my fans at the Indy 500 parade in May 2005.

am just not supposed to father a child. Maybe the vision was about an adopted child. I've got plenty of kids around me. But Laura cuts out her light cigarette habit and her heavier caffeine habit. She knows that she is going to have a baby.

May in Indianapolis is THE month for all good Hoosiers. It's race time. And like all good Hoosier boys I managed to find a way to go to the race for free. I work behind the scenes doing utility work dragging cables and equipment for ABC. And I make extra money. The $500 a month—even with the little extra I get from the Dawn Project working with my kids— isn't really enough to take care of us, so I take on every extra job I can. Whether it's a home rehab or this.

During a day off from the track, I'm doing some rehab work when Laura shows up at the work site and tells me she's pregnant. I'm overwhelmed. I'm thrilled. I also am a little scared since we don't have health insurance. The church doesn't provide coverage with the job, and Laura hasn't worked long enough at the fitness center to have it kick in there. This is still a really good thing. I've gotten through a whole lot of bigger challenges. I stop smoking.

But within two weeks, Laura miscarries. It's awful. I buy a pack of cigs, Laura has a double latte, and we both go into a period of grief. I know that it's my fault—the something in me that's not meant to be a father.

Then after two or three months, Laura discovers that she is pregnant again. On top of that, during that time, her insurance at work has begun, so the entire pregnancy will be covered. I don't mean to think of the miscarriage as a blessing, but had she been pregnant when the insurance kicked in, it would have been considered a pre-existing condition, and nothing would have been covered. Whatever part of the universe looks out for me was doing its thing. A little harshly, but ultimately for the better.

As Laura's pregnancy grows, I start to panic. How am I going to take care of a baby on top of all the other responsibilities and expenses I already have? I'm barely breaking even in a good month. Every negative feeling I've ever had about myself starts to surface. I'm not supposed to be a daddy. I'm going to be a bad daddy. I can't take care of myself, so for sure I can't take care of a whole family.

In her sixth month, Laura quits her job. She has terrible sciatica, a pinched nerve, and just can't keep up with the work and her pregnancy.

I get even more scared. What are we going to do without her insurance coverage? I sink into a deep depression.

I want to die. I know that Laura and the baby will be better without me. I know her parents will take care of them. It's that little kid feeling of wanting to just run away. I stop caring even about my snakes. The rodents I raise as food for them start dying. The snakes are sick. The smell of death starts to fill the house. It's a terrible thing for a home that should be getting ready for a new life.

I confide in Georgette that I'm a mess and don't know what to do. She steps up to the plate and pays for the extended coverage so Laura will still be insured through the birth. That's a huge weight off my shoulders, and I start to turn around.

Raya and I showing off Wally, our alligator, to some of our friends in our living room in 2003.

Indy calendars are really built around May. May of '98 is when Laura first told me she was pregnant. May of '99 is approaching, and that's when she is due. Race time is like the Indy New Year. I start to get hopeful again. The race will bring me the extra work, and I have become the "go to" guy on the job. I know the track inside and out. That responsibility and expertise bolsters my self-esteem. I'm starting to feel better about myself and my world. The first call-day is scheduled for May 13, and I am really looking forward to it.

I arrive at the track and get a call from Laura. Her water broke, and she's in labor. Sometimes my work ethic is way too overdeveloped. Maybe it's a fear of being fired. Maybe it's part of that need for approval. But I tell Laura that I'll be there after 5:00. We'd been to the Lamaze classes, I'd worked in a hospital, and I know—or want to believe—that I have plenty of time. She can't believe her ears. She tells me that she needs me now—not after work. I don't think about it anymore. I go.

I am right there with her when at 9:07 p.m. this perfect baby girl is born. Raya Felice Boneham. Seven pounds, thirteen ounces. Eighteen inches long. And I got to wipe her down right as she comes into the world.

A new RFB is born. We picked the name Raya after Rhea, who in Greek mythology was the daughter of Gaia, Mother Earth, and who became the mother of Zeus, king of the gods. Felice comes from the Italians and means fortunate, but it was really just a name that we liked. My baby girl is RFB the Third.

Every daddy says that becoming a father changes everything. It's true. It changes who you are. Holding that precious newborn—the child of Laura and me, the perfect expression of our love for each other and how that created a new life—

Me on the sidelines operating the boom for a college football game.
(2000)

totally transformed me. All the negative past vanished, and there was only a joyful, proud present.

Naturally I went to work the next day. I had a Polaroid picture of Raya in my hand, and I think I showed it to everyone

The last house that I worked on with my kids group before going away. This is the house before we got started on it in 2000.

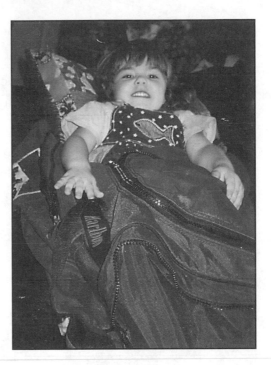

Raya when she emptied my suitcase because she was going with me on my trip.

at the track. "I'm a daddy! This is my baby girl! Isn't she beautiful!"

In anticipation of the birth, I bought a brand new Ford F-150. It was the first new vehicle I had ever owned. I went to the hospital and picked up my new family in my new truck, and we drove to our home. It was my proudest moment.

In Raya's earliest days, I would lay her on my chest and just feel her perfection. I could have stayed like that forever. In December of '99 that dream appears possible when the church tells me that my job at the cemetery is mine for as long as I want to keep it.

Raya loves the outdoors as much as I do. I show her the little fishing hole, and she is able to catch fish as soon as she is walking. She collects flowers and brings them home to Laura. Life is damn near perfect.

A month later, January of 2000, the church turns control of the cemetery over to a private company. I am given notice and six weeks to move out.

I give the tenants who are now living in the Guilford house two weeks to move out and into the duplex. I make the house livable. Rustic. Under construction. But nice. Laura is dreading moving back to the 'hood. For whatever reason, even though it feels like we're moving backwards, I am strangely optimistic. I know that everything is going to work out. My family will be OK. Life goes on.

Raya and me in the big truck getting ready for a picnic at a rest stop.

Raya, just before we left the ABC football tour in 2003.

ABC offers me a job for the college football season. From September to December, I drive the follow-truck that carts stuff along with the rest of the caravan. After I unload the truck, I drive the sideline vehicle. At each game I'm the one driving the boom that holds a camera guy 10 feet in the air. I go back and forth along the sideline and follow the play. I like it. It's TV. The best part is that I can take my wife and daughter with me. It's a working vacation with my family. By now Raya understands that every day you go to work.

When we get back, I can deal with my kids fresh and rejuvenated. We all bond even tighter. They come with me everywhere. Holidays are spent at my house or with Laura's family.

In February 2005, ABC calls and offers me a job working on the Homestead Race, an Indy Racing League event in Homestead, Florida, just outside of Miami. I take two guys with me in my truck, and we head south. Things are about to change, and I'm going to have to leave the mentoring group behind for awhile.

I start telling my kids they need to find another program. I know I'm going to be away, and I don't want them to flounder. I manage to get another mentor started and send him a couple of my kids.

I know that I will be coming back, and I am already starting to make plans filled with high hopes for when I return.

Fame

12

Maybe, one day I'll be able to tell you about this part of my life.....

These pages left
intentionally blank

These pages left
intentionally blank

These pages left
intentionally blank

Now I'm a Celebrity

I've survived my time away from my family. I decide this is a good time for us to take a vacation.

Laura's parents have a place in Labelle, Florida, and it's a perfect retreat for us. It's sort of a retirement trailer-park village. The owner of the park also owns a hotel, and he gives us a room for free. I'm not just the Tyner's son-in-law anymore—I'm Rupert.

While I'm there, I hear from the Autorama Championship Auto Show people who want me to make a personal appearance at their show in Waco, Texas. They will send me a limo, fly me out, and get me home by limo the next day. They are going to pay me money to just show up and sign autographs.

Thousands of people are in line. It's totally outrageous. They have been waiting hours just to see me. I am so pumped up.

For four solid hours, I shake hands, write my name, and jump up and down—on and off the stage—so people can take pictures with me. It's constant motion.

The next day when I wake up, I am actually sore from all that exercise. I had done four hours of high impact aerobics. I was discovering a whole new world.

The next week I was booked for a show in Wichita Falls, Texas. The same thing happens. Thousands of people who just want to meet me. It's like my fan mail has come to life. I get to hear their beautiful stories, their heartbreaking stories, and their touching stories. I am getting all this loving. I am getting paid to do nothing else but just be me.

We are back home in Indianapolis for the next three months. It's time for me to just be at home with my family.

I use the time to try and get through the fan mail. But for every five I answer, twenty more are coming in. I responded to their letters and referred to something in them so everyone would know that I actually read their letter and I was really writing to them. Not some form letter, but a personal one. Being dyslexic it takes me twice as long to write even a short note. It was exhausting. No matter how many I wrote, it looked like I hadn't even made a dent in the pile.

Every letter I get is still sent a handwritten response on my steno pad. It may be only a few words. But it's really me writing back. People have showed me that they have framed the letter I sent them back.

Meanwhile, the neighborhood is noticing me. I had created the image of being the big hairy-scary guy. Some of the 'hood thought I was a cop and that my kids were a chain gang. I encouraged that myth. But now my cover is blown. They know I'm a softie.

By March, our cars have been broken into. Then our garage gets burglarized. I don't want confrontation; I just want it to stop. But people drive by and just sit in their cars in front of my house. Or stand across the street. My family is getting scared. My way of dealing is to go up to them and ask what they want. Pictures? Autographs? I offer to do that for them but tell them that they have to stop. This is reality. I'm real. My wife and daughter are real. You're scaring them. I still have enough scary man inside me that I can look them deep in the eyes, drop my voice, and tell them, "I will protect them." The response is usually one of apology. Sometimes they're just freaked and run away.

A lot of my kids want to prove to their friends that they know me. Some of my friends and family want other people to know that they know me. I arrange to have a weekly event at the Holiday Inn. I am learning that just showing up someplace is worth favors, money, and barters.

I am also learning how to be a celebrity. It's another role to play. Not that it's all that different from me, but there's no down time. I have to be upbeat and pleasant and nice. To everyone. Everywhere. I have to keep giving out love and be happy to take it from anyone who just comes up to say hello.

I've been lucky. I've never had a single negative fan letter. I've never been threatened or jeered at by some hostile drunk who thinks he's better than me or who wants to pick a fight to prove something. At worst, I get people who are overzealous in their love for me, and I have to tell them to calm down. I still don't want confrontation, but I'm not going to run either.

I spent too many years running because that's what I thought I was supposed to do. Now that I've come into my own, I don't want to run from anyone ever again. I have to tell some of them, very nicely, "Thank you. Now go away, or I will have to kill you." And then I smile.

We take a trip to New York City and stay at the Le Parker Meridien Hotel on 57th Street. It's a super fancy-pants kind of place. Next door to Carnegie Hall. All the staff is so formal and polite saying, "Good Morning, Mr. Boneham." "Yes, Mr. Boneham." It's really nice. Way nicer than I am used to.

Everyone tells me that New Yorkers are jaded and cynical and see celebrities all the time so I shouldn't expect anything. That was just too big a challenge. We go to Times Square. Thousands of people navigate through the streets on foot. I stand at the corner of 42nd Street and Broadway—the heart of it all, the damn crossroads of the world—and yell, "I LOVE NEW YORK!" I throw my arms up and growl, "Aargh!" Immediately, I am just mobbed. I have now managed to stop traffic at the busiest intersection in the country, in a place where I was told I would be ignored. I have arrived!!

While we're in New York, Raya turns five. She's crying. She's scared. For years she wanted to go to school, and we told her that she would go when she turned five. Here it is. It's her fifth birthday and we're in New York City. My poor baby thinks she's going to have to stay in New York and go to school here. I calm her down and tell her, "No, Baby, you're not starting school today. We're going to go home. It's OK." It's very grounding. It reminds me of what's really important. We are going to go home. It is all OK.

Our Band of Three

14

I decide to focus on the important things and want to do them right. I open a 529 savings plan for Raya's college education fund. I did my research and found the right one with the best growth, so that when the time comes, she will be able to go to any college in the world. I've told her that, and she knows that her college future is secure. I have always saved for that. Even if I could only put aside five dollars I wanted to make sure that Raya would have a good education. I may have balked at Roger and Georgette's forcing education on me, but I also learned the hard way that it's better to work from the neck up. I make sure that my baby will be able to do that.

Next it's Laura's turn. I tell her that she can have anything she wants. I mean anything. She had worked so hard, put up with so much, that I would have bought her the Taj Mahal if I could. She asks for LASIK eye surgery. She is done with con-

Raya and me in the Union Chapel Cemetery.

tacts. We find a really good doc and make the appointment. This costs only $3,000. Hardly the Taj Mahal, but it's what she wanted.

I write a $100,000 check to Choices, the umbrella organization that has been sending kids to me. With their help, and a bunch of lawyers and accountants, Rupert's Kids gets incorporated as a legitimate 501(c)(3) tax-free charitable institution. For 14 years I had been mentoring as I went along, doing whatever it took to help my kids, including going into debt along the way. Now I can do it the right way and, I believe, make this group the model from which we can grow across the country. There are kids being thrown away everywhere, and this is the start of changing the whole way that society treats them.

We've become a country that believes in tough love, zero tolerance, punishment, three strikes and you're out. The treatment we give these kids with anger issues is to incarcerate them, which simply feeds the anger. These kids have been dealt a rotten hand, haven't had any modeling, nurturing, or love—tough or otherwise. The system treats those delinquents even worse and then they end up in prison. The system gives up on them so early and they remain abandoned forever. They become lifetime offenders.

Rupert's Kids never gives up on anyone. You get as many chances as you need. For as long as it takes. If a kid needs 1,000 strikes over 10 years, he can have them. If he screws up, there are consequences. Sometimes it's jail because that's what he's earned, and part of growing up is facing up to your mistakes. But when he comes out, he comes back and we pick up again.

It's our job to show him that he can have a better life if he's willing to work for it. Most of them aren't willing when I start. They see no value in themselves and no way out, so why try? I show them that there is a way out but it's going to be a lot of hard work.

I show up for them. If I have to go to their houses and get them out of bed at 7:00 a.m., take them to work, and stay with them until I tuck them in at night, that's what I do. They have to know I mean what I say and I say what I mean. And I'm not giving up on them—no matter what.

We can empower those kids, and they will contribute to society, or we can throw them away, and we will have to pay for their care for the rest of their lives.

I know it works.

Martin came to us after he'd been thrown out of every program. He was 300 pounds, had a sixth-grade education, and tested way below the standard on IQ tests. But little by little, we got him to see that he was worth something. There was value just in being Martin.

He came to work and discovered all sorts of things about his own abilities. He can fix things. A big kid can command authority if he does it correctly. On one occasion he was really put to the test.

My kids were working with someone I was trying out as a possible mentor. One of the struggles of Rupert's Kids is finding the right people. I used to think that anyone could do it. After all, if I can be a mentor, anyone can. But I've learned that not everyone can walk into the 'hood and pick up a kid out of his bed when he doesn't want to get up and his parents don't care one way or another. Not everyone can work alongside a group of rowdy big boys and not get intimidated. Sometimes really scary things can happen.

The kids were working on the Guilford House that I had donated to Rupert's Kids so they could have a training site. There they can learn sheetrocking, plastering, plumbing, electrical work, whatever. If they screw it up, they knock it down and start over. No deadlines.

There they are, working away with a possible mentor, when a gang of kids from the 'hood bursts in and holds them up at gunpoint. Everyone is told to give over their money, wallets, cell phones, whatever, and lie face down. Martin, who everyone thought was hopeless, has the presence of mind to tuck his phone into a roll of his belly fat and give up everything else. When the gang leaves, Martin pulls out his cell phone, calls 911, and tells them that Rupert's Kids were just held up on Guilford. The Indianapolis Police Department, who usually ignored the 'hood, showed up and within four hours, the kids had been caught, and the property returned. Thanks to Martin.

Now, the mentor was freaked, and Martin was a hero. The mentor left the program, but Martin has gone on to figure out how to build computer motherboards from spare parts. He's in line to be a Junior Mentor, something he really wants. I told him if he gets his GED, he can become one. Now he has goals, skills, and a future that he looks forward to. He goes to work because he has a reason to work and something to work for.

That's just one story about one kid. Each kid has his own story. I know that this is the way to change society, one kid at a time. Now I believe I have the resources and opportunity to get that going.

Once I incorporate I can actually hire a staff. Incorporation requires a board of directors, and Georgette becomes chairwoman of the board. With her education, her background, and experience, she is perfect for the job.

I ask Victoria Olsen from the Dawn Project to become our director. She's 5 feet, 2 inches tall and will fearlessly walk into any hobo village to find the kid who needs help. She's not only director, but she's also our office manager, caseworker, home-based counselor, and liaison to other agencies. She even goes out on the work crews as a mentor when needed.

Choices recommends that I hire Andy. He looks to be 6 feet, 2 inches and 240 pounds. Size can be an asset in dealing with some of our kids. Andy comes to us more as a computer guy than a mentor, but he says he will try mentoring along with his other duties. I always hold out hopes that someone can become a mentor. It's a critical role that allows us to expand.

Unlike Georgette, Victoria and Andy don't have any letters after their names. I don't either. That's part of how it works. Rupert's Kids puts the value in people and experience—not degrees, positions, or even history, as long as they aren't a danger to the organization or its members.

Everyone I work with has to go by one simple rule. Mean what you say and say what you mean. With integrity, a good heart, and the desire to help, there's a place for you.

Our band of three starts to make a go of it. But it's a struggle in every way. Volunteers appear but stop showing up once they've met me. Not that I scare them away (or maybe I do), it's just that some people come only to meet Rupert and not to really work. The same thing happens with some of the corporations. They show up but forget their checkbooks. It's frustrating, but I tell my team that it will all work out. I have faith that the Great Spirit will deliver answers. As well as money and people.

We launch our websites, www.RupertsKids.org and www.RupertsKids.com, and some donations start coming in. We get a couple of $1,000 gifts, but most of them are just a few dollars. In some ways, those are the ones that mean the most to me. There's a nine-year-old boy from Las Vegas who for the past two years has given $5 a week and has promised to keep that up for as long as he possibly can. He recently told me that his allowance has increased and he'll be giving more. His parents send us a check every month as well.

But we're struggling. We now have an organization with expenses and we need support. Our operating budget is laughably small, but it still requires money. And we really need people to help in the office and especially to become mentors. That's key. In the months where we don't make our expenses, I write a check to cover it, but I can't just create new mentors.

For a while we invent the program as we go, creating, changing, modifying our construction crew. At the same time we are trying to get my mission statement down on paper, create websites, and apply for our 501(c)(3). There are a lot of things involved in starting a new non-profit! It's the way I've always worked, constantly trying to improve the mentoring program to fit the needs of the kids we serve. We can't really take kids directly out of the court system yet. We're too new and don't have a track record. Our staff doesn't hold a lot of degrees and credentials.

We still don't have a full-time mentor. In December 2004, Rupert's Kids receives its nonprofit status from the federal government and the Internal Revenue Service. About six months after that, another blessing comes our way. John, a 46-year-old AmeriCorps worker, becomes part of our team. He has office skills, construction knowledge, and mentoring ability. His modest stipend comes through AmeriCorps, a national organization whose structure supports people who want to give back for a year's commitment. This is exactly what we needed—our own mentor.

Now we are on a mission. With a few of the guys from my old program who are still struggling, our volunteers, and our new mentor, we are up and running!

Then Lindsey Purcell from the Arbor Division of the Indianapolis Parks and Recreation Department appears. He proposes that the kids start taking care of the parks rather than just working on rehab construction. Anyone can push a damn lawnmower. I've had landscaping experience from back when I took care of the cemetery. I can teach this. Lindsey is willing to help train as well.

Me and some old friends at a fundraiser for Rupert's Kids. (Photo by Jimmy Swan)

I immediately know that this is a great idea. We can adopt parks. We can take care of the ignored parks in the forgotten parts of the city and make them nice. We can save the city a bundle because they won't have to hire crews to maintain those places, and show the value in our kids. We can teach work ethic, pride in completing work, and community service. All in one job.

First, we have to prove ourselves to the city.

Lindsey and Rupert's Kids make a deal with the parks department for Rupert's Kids to participate in the city's annual Christmas Tree Recycling Program.

Every year, from January through March, Indianapolis asks people to bring their Christmas trees to various park loca-

Meet one of Rupert's Kids
Melvin

Little Melvin is 15 when he comes to me. It's the late 1990s, and he is living at a state hospital as an in-patient. He's been through the juvenile court system for vandalism, breaking and entering, and other assorted petty crimes. He's been diagnosed as mentally handicapped with an IQ of 62 and is a ward of the state, having been taken away from unfit parents.

In an effort to "mainstream" him, the system has decided that he can go to public school for one class—gym. He changes before he leaves. They bus him to school. He stays in his gym clothes till he comes back. He is totally isolated from any of the kids and has no socialization with anyone in the public schools.

His grandparents are willing to take him in. Our goal is to get him back into school and back into life. I still remember Victoria, the director of Rupert's Kids, and I standing up saying we will take him and create a 24-hour program of "wrap-around services" that will include school and work.

For the first month I keep him with me seven days a week from 7:00 a.m. until 7:00 p.m. I tell him that until he goes back to school, he goes to work. I take him to the YMCA and teach him how to work out so he can get more comfortable in his body. I take him to a restaurant so he can learn how to order off a menu. (I have to prime the waitress first, but there's always a cute one who wants to help.) He has to learn almost every practical behavior skill for day-to-day life.

131

After three or four months I'm taking Melvin to school half of the day and to work the other half. We manage to get him industrial arts credit for his work time.

He starts taking the bus to school on his own. For the first few weeks I drive by the bus stop to make sure he's there, and then I park out of sight to watch him get on the bus.

He starts going to school full-time and working afternoons and weekends.

He graduates from a regular public high school. He's got a job as a cashier and is making his own way.

tions to be recycled into mulch. Through Lindsey we work with the parks department so that Rupert's Kids will be able to participate as a work crew. There are five parks where trees are collected.

At first, the city crew doesn't want the kids anywhere near the actual chipper. It's potentially a very dangerous piece of equipment. Fine. There's a huge pile of trees so they start by just dragging one tree at a time from the pile to the machine.

After a couple of hours seeing what hard workers these kids are, the city crew starts to let them join in. Not only dragging the trees but feeding them into the chipper as well. Pretty soon they are turning huge piles of trees into truckloads of mulch.

That year, there were a thousand more trees dropped off into the parks then there ever had been before. Because of the kids' hard work, the project finished six weeks earlier than ever before. My kids got more done in less time.

With success like that, we are able to start our Adopt-A-Park Program. We pick three parks and the city picks three. We agree to do all the maintenance—mowing, cleaning, weeding, whatever. We have over 16 acres of park ground to care for.

The word is out that we have room for more kids and new ones come our way. We've got a few home lawn mowers, some tools, and my truck to transport the crew and equipment in. We go to work. It's brutally hard pushing those home mowers around. After the first mow, we spring for four self-propelled mowers. It's still killer work, but what an improvement.

It's a huge challenge keeping these kids involved and wanting to do the work.

We try to make it fun. Even when it's backbreaking. When you push a mower for hours, your hands swell up so bad you can't snap your fingers. We try to make that a game. "Bet you can't snap your fingers." When they show up the next day, we'll ask, "Can you snap your fingers, yet?" It's silly, but it lets them know you understand just how hard they are working. So hard that their hands are suffering. Just using their hands is work.

We tell them how strong they are getting. That this kind of work is building up their muscles and their minds. The kids start to notice how the other kids are developing, and they don't want to be left behind.

They begin to really see what a difference each one of them is making. When a new kid drops a candy wrapper one of the others will yell at him to pick it up. They have an emotional investment and pride in their work. They develop pride in their community. Most importantly, they start taking pride in themselves.

Meet one of Rupert's Kids
Devon

Devon came to me before I even went away. He's autistic and was struggling in high school, special education classes, and every other program they put him in or threw him out of. He's diagnosed emotionally handicapped and lives in a totally dysfunctional household.

When he first came to me, he was so painfully shy he couldn't look anyone in the face. I had to drag him to work for the first month or so, and he would just sit in the truck and watch the others. That's pretty common.

Gradually he decides he wants to be part of the team and he starts joining in. Before too long he's working really hard.

We get him back into public school full time, and then I go away. But before I leave I look him in the eye and say, "Devon, TRY and make it through this last year. You can do it. Just try."

Sure enough when I get back he's graduated. In fact, he's accepted into Indiana University-Purdue University Indianapolis (IUPUI) and living in the dorms.

But he has a setback. The university gave him all his scholarship money in a lump sum and he's gone through it and doesn't know what to do. He comes back to Rupert's Kids for help. Any kid can always come back to us for help any time they need it.

We put him to work in the office. Stuffing envelopes. Answering the phone. Filing. He even helps on the construction crew and the park crews. We teach him about saving and budgeting. I show him how I managed to live on next to nothing when I had to.

Devon is now in his sophomore year of college. He's still not sure what he wants to do but he's taking a lot of general studies classes for now. The autistic kid that wasn't supposed to make it living on his own, has a girlfriend, and sees a real future for himself.

While I was writing this book, Melvin falls back through the cracks. I hope he is able to come back to Rupert's Kids when he can.

On a better note, Martin, the kid who called 911 and saved the day when we were being robbed, is now working as a junior mentor for Rupert's Kids. He is continuing his work toward his GED and encouraging other Rupert's Kids to follow his lead. It's all about the Martins of this world…the more we help them, the more they learn to help themselves.

Because I'm "Rupert," Rupert's Kids has gotten some public attention. With that has come some corporate sponsorship. I'm really grateful to companies like Hardee's, GasAmerica, and the Indianapolis Motor Speedway, who have all given thousands to help Rupert's Kids. And I'm really excited that Toro is donating two commercial mowers. That's going to make an enormous difference in the work we can do.

Rupert's Kids is making a difference. In our community and with our kids. We are breaking the cycles of abuse where all they have learned is aggression. Instead of locking our kids up for acting out on that learned behavior, we show each one of them that there is a better way. We create a program that will work for each kid because each one of them is unique. And they need that unique identity affirmed and supported. Their model has been people screwing them—literally or figuratively—their whole lives. We teach them not to give up and just say, "Screw it!" We teach them that life is good, it is ok to be you, and it is a great thing to give back.

Like the old saying, we're "teaching a kid to fish." And they will teach others. One kid at a time, we will change the system, and I truly believe, we will change the world.

Rupert, Inc.

15

People are starting to change around me. Friends, my more extended family, even my old buds start treating me differently. They want to do things for me. Make sure I'm taken care of. People want to claim a stake in the life of someone they see as famous.

The only people who don't change is my family and my kids. But even they can get caught up in it. If I take my kids to an event appearance, they can get carried away and start asking for a picture and an autograph. I have to remind them, "Hey, we already have pictures of us together."

The neighborhood certainly sees me differently. They see a big dollar sign on my door as if I'm keeping all my money in the house somewhere. Our garage is broken into twice. Then they break into the house. I'm not sure, but it may have even happened while we were upstairs sleeping. We start packing. We'll live at the Holiday Inn till we can find a new house.

There isn't a whole lot to pack. Most of the stuff in the house is found. Stuff I rescued from the street. I don't need to take someone's used couch with me. What I do pack are my treasures. My Winnie the Pooh doll I've had since I was a kid. My collections of rocks and skulls. My Sagamore Stick. Even when I was living in my car, I managed to hold on to these few special things.

People don't seem to know how to behave around me. As we're packing up the truck, some of the neighborhood starts to gather around the house. No one offers to help, mind you. It's raining, and they just stand there and watch Laura and me carry boxes. One guy knocks into Laura as she is carrying out boxes, and the stuff inside spills into a puddle. This kind of insane behavior scares her.

My first instinct is to protect Laura. I ask him what he's doing. Once again, he's just some fan who wants a picture and an autograph. I tell him he can have all he wants, but then he's going to have to go. I'm picking my stuff up out of water, and he is still standing there. I am beginning to understand that fans are oblivious to reality. They really don't mean any harm—usually—but some of them just don't know how to behave. They are in awe because they are standing next to somebody they think is a celebrity. Every day I get another lesson in being a celebrity. What it means. How to act it. It's a full-time job.

We go house hunting in Laura's old neighborhood. It's a nice part of town. Not super-rich mansions, not trendy, not fancy-pants, just nice. It will be a sweet neighborhood to come home to and a safe and comfortable one for my family.

We look at one house. For sale by owner. I am offering cash. I want a house. Right now. The first guy doesn't want to meet our terms, and they are pretty easy. I need him out of the house in three days.

The second house we look at, I make the same offer. We negotiate in the driveway. No realtors. No lawyers. I'll write a check, and you move out in three days. He agrees.

Raya's own publicity photo for all of my autograph signings. (2004)

It has taken all of a month to come home, to spend some money, to buy a house, and to move out of the Guilford dump and into our nice, new home. I'm tired.

We move in with practically nothing but some clothes and an air mattress to sleep on. It's still so much better than anything we've ever had before. It's a sweet ranch-style home with plenty of room for my family and my pets. There's a backyard and small stream that runs along the property lines. I can still remember when my highest priority was to find a place with a toilet so I could take a dump inside. Now I'm a homeowner in a nice neighborhood and a celebrity that people will wait hours to meet.

My first hometown appearance comes at Hoosier Park, the local harness racetrack, on May 29, 2004. I'm back in Indianapolis for less than a month now. I was so busy getting my new life together and dealing with the 'hood's response, that I was not prepared for what was out there waiting for me.

I had signed to do a four-hour "meet and greet." I arrive around sundown, and there are thousands—thousands!—of people waiting to shake my hand and get an autograph. They'd been lining up for hours. It's the biggest turnout they have ever had in a single day.

It's an extreme high. People oozing love. I am meeting my fans, and they come in all shapes, sizes, and ages. Guys who want to be me. Kids who think I'm a hero. Twenty-year-old girls who think I'm cool and 80-year-old grandmas who giggle and blush when I give them a hug. Each one with another story—thrilling, sad, gut wrenching, heartwarming, beautiful stories. Telling me why their stories are important to them. "My mother on her deathbed said to tell you how happy you made her," said one fan. I am learning that being a celebrity means you are not just someone people see at events, you are an important part of their lives. Crazy. But I am thrilled with every minute of it.

After four hours, the line has barely moved. They ask me to stay longer. Things are out of control. I have been signing as fast as I possibly can, and there are still thousands more who want to meet me. They don't offer any more money for my extra time. That is a lesson I was still learning: Being a celebrity is not just a status but also a job, and it can be a pretty well-paying one if you work it right.

I stay until nearly 2:00 a.m. Eight hours of nonstop signing as fast as I can go. It was exhausting, gratifying, and thrilling. Things were just starting to take off.

The next day is the parade that kicks off the Indy 500. They put me on my own float where I get to ride with my wife and daughter. At first, Raya doesn't want any part of this. When she is certain she can hide behind Laura and me if she needs to, she agrees. She ends up having a great time. From that point on, whenever she hears that I'm doing a parade, she wants to know what kind of float she will be riding on.

The race is the single biggest event in Indianapolis. Half-a-million people from everywhere fill the track. For so many years, I had worked the race with the camera crews as a grip, but now, I am asked to join the VIPs who ride around the track before the race in what they call the "Celebrity Lap." The bigwigs who have come to the race are introduced, and they walk out on the track. Then they get in a car that rides one lap around the entire track.

Me and my family at the 2006 Indianapolis 500 Festival Parade. (Photo by Jimmy Swan)

My name is announced, and I head out toward the celebrity vehicle. The ground itself shakes with the deafening roar. I am screaming. The fans are cheering. I feel all this power and love. We drive around the two-and-a-half miles of track, and I am on top of the world.

Every TV camera is focused tight on me. The crew, the techies, and the directors are all my buddies, and they are making sure I get maximum coverage. A year ago I was working with them, and now they've got their cameras trained on me in a close-up.

At the end of the loop, the announcer says, "We love Rupert! I have never heard anyone get a response like that from the crowd." It gets even louder as I head off to the celebrity suite to watch the race. For a Hoosier boy, it doesn't get any better than this.

June comes and it's Father's Day. I hadn't spoken to Roger for a couple of years. He showed up when Raya was born and for her third birthday. He and his new wife come into Indianapolis from Bloomington a lot for all sorts of reasons, but they never come by. They say it's because they don't like spending time in Indianapolis. Of course, they don't call and arrange to meet us someplace else either.

Roger had been talking about me to *The National Enquirer*. For "Rupert's Secret Wife," he told them about my previous common-law marriage. "Rupert's Strange Fetish" was a story about my skull collection, many of which he had given me as a kid to encourage me to be a scientist. All basically true stuff but twisted and told in that creepy *Enquirer* way, and all validated by an unimpeachable source: Rupert's father.

I'm really not angry over it. It's Roger. He never knew how to be the father I needed. Why should things be different now? But I call. I'm in a pretty good place at this point. I think that

143

I can handle whatever. He spends an hour yelling at me for making him look like an idiot by not telling him what I was doing. He doesn't want to know anything about my life, but now I'm at fault for not keeping him up to date. He tells me what a thoughtless son I am and asks how could I do this to him.

We don't speak again until my daughter's sixth birthday a year later, when Roger shows up to drop off a present for Raya. When he leaves, he asks me to walk him out. He said, "You know I'm proud of you" in a hard, Roger tone. Not knowing what to say, I respond, "I know." I haven't talked to him since. I really don't know what to say to him.

Right away, I can see how upside down my world has become. It hasn't improved my relationship with my brother, my sister-in-law, or my mother. It sure hasn't changed a damn thing between Roger and me—maybe it's made things worse. I also see the toll it's already taking on my own family.

Laura is starting to get depressed. I was away for so long, and now I'm going out on appearances. When we're home, we can't go anywhere because we get mobbed, and Laura hates crowds.

My baby is seeing how the crowds are taking away her daddy time, and she hates it. We used to go to the zoo every week, and now it's been like a year since we've gone. One rainy day I decide that we'll go. I figure on a bad day there won't be as many people, and we'll have an easier time.

When we get there, people start to follow us, but they sort of tag along around 20 feet away. Raya and I go into the cafeteria to get something to eat. When we try to get out, practically the entire zoo is waiting at the door. They surround us and

Fishing at my favorite fishing hole in 2005.

back us up to the petting zoo. We are trapped. They are all saying, "Hey, Rupert!" or "We love you, Rupert!" All good stuff, but it's loud. There's a whole lot of them and only two of us. My baby is getting scared, "Make 'em stop, Daddy!"

I get loud. "You're scaring my kid, and we're done. You gotta stop and leave us alone." But they are insistent. "Just a picture." "Just an autograph." They won't stop.

I take out my cell phone and call the zoo office. I get transferred to security and tell them what's going on and that we need help. The zoo has to dispatch a security team to come rescue us, take us out a back exit, and escort us to our car.

I have to explain to Raya that our world is different now. There are no strangers. People know my favorite color, my favorite foods, and my pets' names. They know her pets' names. If anyone tries to tell her they are a friend of Daddy's, no matter what they seem to know, don't believe it.

I don't want to scare her, so I don't say they could be predators. I just tell her that those are fans not friends, and she should never go off with any fan. How weird is it that when we lived in the 'hood surrounded by junkies and thieves, we created a safe little bubble for ourselves. Now I really need that fortress of solitude, and it's a lot harder to maintain.

In our nice, new neighborhood, people are hanging around our house all the time. Little girls gather in the driveway. Daddies walk with their kids along the little stream just behind my house. I don't really blame them. I probably would have done the same thing, too, if a celebrity moved into my neighborhood. Especially when I was a kid.

But it forces me to build a small privacy fence on part of my backyard. At first Laura doesn't want me to do it. Nobody else has a fence. But I need a place where I can go outside with my daughter, Raya, and play in the sandbox. I want to hang out without worrying that someone is going to snap a picture or just intrude on my private time.

I am learning very quickly that I have to keep grounded and keep my priorities straight. Nothing, absolutely nothing, is going to mess with my family and my relationship with them.

Between May 2004 and January 2005, I will spend about 200 days on the road. I go from one side of the country to the other. I make sure that if there's any kind of layover time, a break in the day, I can route myself back through Indianapolis and spend time with my wife and daughter.

The entrepreneur in me realizes that with all these requests for appearances I need to build a self-booking business. While I've got all those attorneys working on creating a not-for-profit Rupert's Kids, I have them draw up the papers to create a for-profit side: RFB Enterprises. My daughter thinks this stands for Raya Felice Boneham. She knows it will all be hers someday anyhow. She even has her own office on our site, with a desk and her stuff in it.

It becomes a way to help support myself and my family, and at the same time raise awareness—and money—for Rupert's Kids.

Not only do I do the "meet and greet" gigs, I get commercial appearances. Any company looking for a "feel-good" guy suddenly wants Rupert.

One of the deals I sign is with Dodge & Miller Racing. They have their Raminator at Monster Truck shows. They create the Dodge "Rupert" Raminator as part of the show and I get to drive it at different events across the country. My favorite time was at the RCA Dome in Indianapolis. I was able to crush a pile of cars, then jump halfway out the window and scream while pyrotechnics were firing off behind me. It was a great feeling to have 20,000 fans yelling and screaming with me.

Sometimes I can't believe how much plain, old fun being me can be.

Then I start going out on motivational speaking talks.

I go to the National Deli Association Meeting. Three hundred men and women in suits who have never heard of me. I get up in my usual tie-dye tank top and cargo shorts and they have no idea what the hell I'm doing there. I start making references to things about me that I think everybody knows, and it gets no response. I learn that you can't make assumptions about who you're talking to. But I can be me and talk to them about what I know.

I talk to them about the same things I tell my kids. It's just a different perspective. I talk about ethical business practices.

I remind them that you can sometimes achieve rewards by screwing the little guy. But you don't get away with it more than one or two times. And you don't have to do it at all. It's always better to create deals where both sides walk away feeling like winners. Turn "you against me" into "you and I can…"

Build a reputation on the same principles I teach my kids. "Mean what you say, and say what you mean." People will hear about your reputation and they will seek you out because they know they don't have to worry about getting screwed.

These suits are starting to listen. In a little over an hour they have gone from sitting there looking at me like some freak, into a group of people laughing and cheering me on.

One of them comes up to me afterwards to thank me. He tells me that the biggest thing he learned from the speech—

aside from what I said—was how appearances can be so deceiving. He realized that he went from a place of judging me for the way I looked to appreciating me for who I am. In about one hour I've turned a group of corporate suits into a bunch of Rupert's Kids. By just being me.

Letting Go of the Demons and Ghosts

16

Most of the events I go out on are terrific, and I have a great time. The most outrageously fantastic day was in Binghamton, New York, at their Spiedie Fest. A spiedie is marinated meat that's grilled on a skewer and then put into an Italian sandwich roll. The skewer is pulled out, and you've got your spiedie. In August, Binghamton does a huge fair that includes one of the biggest hot-air balloon races in the country.

I am booked for my "meet and greet" from 11:00 a.m. to 3:00 p.m., but I get there at 6:00 a.m. so I can take my first balloon ride. It's kind of scary but really cool. We're flying over the fairgrounds, and I see people lining up. I think this must be some big deal if people arrive at 6:00 a.m. I thought they were lining up to get in. What I saw were people lining up to see me.

Talking with a young fan at my first stage show in Warsaw, Indiana, in 2004. (Photo by Jimmy Swan)

Over 25,000 people are waiting for me when I get to my signing station. The promoters have figured out that if I give people 10 seconds, I can shake their hands and sign my picture. No, to anyone's request for anything beyond that. Nothing special. Just a, "Hey, how are ya?" and move them through. At 10 seconds per person, I can go through 350 people an hour. Security is determined to keep it moving.

After I've gone through over a thousand fans, I haven't made a dent. The promoters decide that I won't even sign anything anymore. They take my Sharpie away, and we are going to

At a Home Depot kids workshop in Indianapolis, Indiana, in 2005. (Photo by Jimmy Swan)

walk through the crowd so people can touch me or I can shake a hand as I pass. Two huge guys lead me through the crowd, protecting me. It's outrageous. I am being protected. And I need the help!

There are still 20,000 people waiting for me. They ask me if I will go on the stage where the bands play and talk to the crowd. Hell yes, I will. I get up there and tell stories. I answer some questions. For an hour, I am just me. I love it! They love me! It is the best time ever. I have just done my first "on-stage." I end with a big growl and a huge, "I love you guys." The crowd yells back, and the roar actually shakes the stage under my feet. I never want to leave.

At the other end of the spectrum was a charity weekend in Columbus, Indiana. I hadn't yet learned how to help people promote an event that I was coming to. These people had heard about all the thousands of fans that have shown up at the other places and assume they will have the same turnout. They didn't realize you have to tell people what's happening. You could have Jesus, Buddha, and Mohammed appearing onstage, but if your only promo was a sign outside saying, "Tonight here: Jesus, Buddha, and Mohammed," no one is going to know about it. If no one knows about it, no one shows up.

About a hundred people found their way to the event. It was pitiful. But it was a really good lesson, too. It reminded me that I can't count on being a celebrity forever. It could all go away in a flash.

In August I was booked for the Haynes-Apperson Festival in Kokomo. Haynes and Apperson invented the internal combustion engine long before Ford or anyone knew what to do with it. Being Kokomo's most famous historical figures, they are celebrated every year with the biggest event on the town's calendar.

In 2004, it became the Rupert-Haynes-Apperson Festival. I rode on a huge float in the big parade. There were articles in the paper about me as a kid. Some people wrote letters of apology to the paper remembering how badly they had treated me in school.

I took my family around to all the sad places of my child-hood. I could feel all the demons and ghosts that haunted me. I showed them the places where I got beat up so many times. And the places that I ran to so I could hide.

I found Amu, who I was the seeing-eye dog for. We had a sweet private reunion at his house.

The hard part was explaining to my daughter why I was so sad. Telling her that her big strong daddy had spent so much of his childhood being weak and afraid. I tried to tell her that it was OK to be scared or weak sometimes. That you can grow and put that stuff behind you. I told her, "I'm just glad that I don't live in that place anymore."

I signed a deal to appear at a car show in Abilene, Texas. As it approached, I dreaded going to Abilene. Kokomo held de-mons of sad times. Abilene was filled with ghosts of people in my life who were all actually dead. Most of them died from alcohol, drugs, or violence. I was both afraid and at the same time hoped that some of those kids I lived with and left be-hind would show up so I could apologize. But they didn't. Diana, the one person in Abilene who really loved me, didn't show either. I guess I was relieved not to have to face her. Who I did meet were a lot of 20-somethings who had pic-tures of me with their parents. They would show me the snap-shot and say, "Isn't that you with my Mom?"

"Yes, do you want me to sign it?"

"Oh sure. That'd be cool."

Throwing out the first pitch for an Indianapolis Indians game in 2004. (Photo by Jimmy Swan)

"How is your mom?"

"She died a few years ago."

I really was staring ghosts in the face. As soon as my time was over, I ran to my hotel and called my family.

Then I spent some time with my one buddy from that era that I was still in touch with, my buddy Jeb. He was an ex-Navy guy who had somehow ended up in the brig. They tortured him there, made him crazy, and then kicked him out of the Navy. He was just the kind of guy I hung with. I managed to help him get on disability, and we stayed friends.

Kokomo and Abilene feel like such a long time ago. It's such an incredible journey—where I came from to where I am. My past is a part of me, but it doesn't control me any more. I have become more than my history. I've always been me. I just had to learn who that is and what he is capable of.

It's the craziest thing for me to use terms like "my fans." To even think about "legions of people who believe in me." Sometimes I start to question it and ask "Why me?" People in my family like Roger or Chris will ask, "Why Rupert?" and encourage my self-doubts. I've learned not to give them the power they once had. I try not to give that power to anyone. Not to the people who don't believe in me and not to those who adore me. Sometimes the question—"Why me?"—loses its power, too. I manage to just accept it with all the other ups and downs.

Living the Good Life

The offers for appearances aren't coming in as often. I don't get as many letters a day, but I am OK with that. I don't need to be a celebrity. My life doesn't hinge on it. It's great fun and I love it, but it doesn't define me.

I realized right from the time I got back, that fame is fleeting and that I couldn't bank on it. I also know that even if people stop wanting me in front of the camera, they will always need cameras, and people behind them, to fill all those stations with all that airtime.

So I started my own production company.

I had worked as the sideline driver for ABC's *Monday Night Football* and the college package. I knew the ropes, and I knew the guys. I always put my faith in people first.

Laura and I before an event in Indianapolis in 2006. (Photo by Jimmy Swan)

Billy Constable and I went back to when I worked at Crackers Comedy Club in Indianapolis. By 1999, he was known as "Cart Boy" for his abilities as a sideline driver. Rob Lombardi was the head utility guy on the Monday night crew and, like me, was the go-to kind of worker. He is the kind of guy who never says, "That can't be done." He figures out how to do it.

I call up these two guys and offer them a partnership in my new company. I've still got that legal and accounting team working on Rupert's Kids and RFB Enterprises, and now they have one more entity to structure. For $500 I'm able to incorporate, and Tournament Towers is launched. I've turned three guys and a truck into a production company.

I put in a bid to ABC for the same package that I had been working for somebody else. They hired us and we're off and running. I expected five years of struggle, like most corporations have in the first years, but Tournament Towers is turning a profit off its first contract.

I run my business with the same principles I've been preaching. When the cost of gas went up, I didn't run to ABC and ask for a "fuel surcharge" the way so many companies were doing. We made a deal for a price, and it was my job to hold to it. As a result, ABC gave us an extension on the contract. Our word makes us more than just another trucking company.

Me at an event in Terre Haute, Indiana, in 2005. (Photo by Jimmy Swan)

At the end of our first season with them, ABC's production manager and technical director said, "We couldn't have done it without you." We were named their, "Most Valuable Little Vendor."

We started with one network covering football. We now have five crews and deals with ABC, ESPN, NBC, and the new NFL Network. My professional crews work the same way my kids do. They give 100 percent effort 100 percent of the time. They are willing to work longer and harder than everyone else to get the job done better and faster and cheaper. They find value in the work itself as a reflection of who they are.

With the not-for-profit and profit entities growing, I realize that I need space to work from. I can't just borrow a desk in the corner of Choices. I have always hated to pay rent. Even when I didn't have any money to buy anything, I bartered my labor for housing.

Having turned around those lost houses in the 'hood, I know something about real estate, so I form one more company: RBRD—Rupert Boneham Realty Development.

I find 10,000 square feet in a beautiful couple of buildings. It's in a good neighborhood, and I can afford it. It's in move-in condition and has a built-in tenant to defray some of the operating costs. RBRD makes its first purchase.

Its first deal as a landlord is to rent space to Rupert's Kids for $1 a year.

Rupert's Kids will always remain my most important work. It continues to grow and serve the community in its unique way. I am determined to take this concept of wraparound, full-service mentoring to cities across the country.

Me live on WSEE 35, a CBS affiliate in Erie, Pennsylvania, in 2005. (Photo by Jimmy Swan)

Another company I am working with is BurnLounge. I have a store for Rupert's Kids that sells music. It can also be a label and worldwide distributor for any of my kids that create their own songs or music. It is at www.burnlounge.com/rupert. It's a cool place to go to download music. What makes it different is that 20 percent of the sales go directly to Rupert's Kids. I keep looking for ways to expand awareness, strengthen support, and generate income so that more kids in more places can be helped.

There are so many kids who have been abandoned by their families and by the system. I refuse to write them all off as

Appearing on WISH-TV Channel 8, a CBS affiliate in Indianapolis, Indiana, in 2005. (Photo by Jimmy Swan)

lost causes. I know they need help, and we all can give them hope. They need mentoring to guide them, so they can discover who they are and what they are capable of doing.

I think I have an idea of what I have given to my fans. They hold the hope that they will behave the way I did. Honorable but not an angel. Basically good but clearly a screw-up at times. Someone who works hard and takes care of the people around him. Someone who trusts his friends even to the point of being stupid. Someone who is not afraid to wear a skirt if that's what makes the most sense. Someone who embraces each experience and plays with all his heart.

People remember me for how I made them feel. They tell me, "You made me laugh so hard." Or, "When you kissed your wife, I cried." And, "When you roared, I felt so excited. I felt like a winner."

People saw me live out the philosophy I tell my kids:

Life is good.

Be you.

Give back.

But what do I know? I'm just being me.

My Book: Just Doing It

Shortly after becoming a celebrity I decide it's time to write a book about my life's journey. I think it may actually have an impact on people who would read it, and realize that no matter how bad things may get you can turn your life around. If I can go from living under a bridge to winning $1,000,000 any one can turn their life around. And who knows, maybe they can win the big prize, too.

I talk to a couple of fancy pants publishers and realize they have little or no interest in me or my book. I also realize they aren't going to pay me anything. I spend the better part of a year trying to get my life down on paper. I find it very hard to sit down and write, as the process causes me to unlock memories and emotions that have been put away for years. With everything in my life now in high gear, the book takes a back seat.

I come up with the idea of doing a kid's coloring and activity book. The fancy pants publishers have no interest, so as far as I am concerned a Rupert book is a dead deal.

As I am walking back to the VIP suites at the 2004 Indy 500 after the parade lap, I am introduced to a guy who owns a local publishing company. Within 30 seconds he says "Rupert you should write a book and let us be your publisher!" He thinks I have the fan base to pull it off. We agree to meet.

At our first meeting I am introduced to everyone. We talk in generalities about the concept, how it would be done, and in general how we would do the business side of it. These guys are much more generous than the fancy pants publishers. Sounds simple enough. But it takes me about a year to decide I can't do it on my own. We agree to hire a writer, Lester, who will interview me and write down what I say. We all sign the contract in November 2005, and begin that same month with the video interviews.

After the video interviews Lester starts writing. For the next six months Lester and I are on the phone or meeting together all the time. The chapters start coming and we seem to have a book. It's now the summer of 2006 and I am getting excited about the fall launch. Then we hit a snag. The corporate powers that be have to review every chapter, and it delays the book until after Christmas. We are all bummed because we are missing the Christmas season but we keep an upbeat attitude.

As fall approaches the book is going through the final editing process and we start to talk to the distributors and bookstores. I am so excited! I cannot wait to do the book signings and be able to connect on a more personal level with my fans.

My book is going to become a reality and I have achieved another life milestone. How far I have come from that darn bridge, I hope you liked it!

More About Rupert and His Organization

Rupert's Kids

If you are already a fan of Rupert Boneham, you may already know that his life is "all about the kids." Rupert has dedicated his life to helping others, especially kids—teens who are "down and out," been given up on, and are headed for more trouble. Rupert's Kids is an organization that Rupert Boneham founded BEFORE he was a celebrity. He has been able to help many children in the Indianapolis area, and now his goal is to help kids *wherever* they live.

Rupert's Kids provides mentoring and educational programming to troubled youth. Part of the program is tough love, but much of it is just plain LOVE. From work programs to teach the value of hard work, to the learning of life's hardest lessons, Rupert pours his heart and soul into every person who goes through his program.

Rupert's Kids serves youth and young adults, ages 18-24, who have already passed through nearly every social service agency in the system. They are typically "last chance" youth who have yet to achieve stable housing and employment. They pass from agency to agency, often returning to the challenges that created the situations they find themselves in now. It is a cycle that, uninterrupted, leads to years of trouble.

Through work, such as landscaping and home renovation, Rupert's Kids teaches life skills that help its youth learn how to be productive members of society. Homes renovated through the program are donated to low-income families, or are used as transitional housing for members of Rupert's Kids.

Rupert often says that "I was one of Rupert's Kids," and in many ways that is very true. He worked to better his life and provide for his family, all while helping others to do the same.

What's in the future for Rupert's Kids? That's partly up to you. The organization is working on implementing and rolling out Rupert's Kids programs in cities nationwide! To do that, they need your help. Your monetary donation will go a long way to making Rupert's Kids an organization that helps kids everywhere become productive members of society! Simply go to www.rupertskids.org and click on the "donate" link at the top of the page. There you will find information about how YOU can help make a difference in the lives of the youth in your community!

Mission Statement

The mission of Rupert's Kids is to empower youth to discover their inner strengths, and realize their own self-worth and their value to society.

The goals of Rupert's Kids:

1. Provide mentoring and educational programming to youth.

2. Develop housing options for low-income families.

3. Foster community partnerships, which serve youth and families.

4. Help provide financial assistance and services to youth, low-income, and homeless families in the areas of education, vocational training, and job placement.

5. Develop committed volunteers and donors to provide time, money, and property.

How to Contact Rupert

You can reach Rupert by one of the following methods:

- By fax: 317-257-4732
- By mail: RFB Enterprises
               737 E. 86th St.
               Indianapolis, Indiana 46240

- By e-mail: Rupert@rupertskids.org

Autographs

Rupert is always happy to autograph items for his fans! Simply send your item, with any autograph instructions, to the address below, with a prepaid return envelope so your item can be returned to you.

RFB Enterprises
737 E. 86th St.
Indianapolis, Indiana 46240

Fan Mail

Rupert loves to receive mail from his fans! You can send to the address below, and be sure to include your name, address, phone number, and email address!

RFB Enterprises
737 E. 86th St.
Indianapolis, Indiana 46240

Teachers! Send Rupert letters from your students and your school! Rupert loves to come and talk with students about how to achieve their goals in life. Let us know how we can help you make your classroom better. We will contact you to see how we can work together!

Order an Autographed Copy of this Book

Order your own autographed copy of *Rupert: Just Being Me* by visiting www.rupertsbook.com.

How to Become a Mentor

Want to help out? Become a mentor with Rupert's Kids! Whether it is a few hours a week or a few days a month, mentors are always needed. All you need is a desire to give back to the community and the ability to model positive behavior, showing our kids how to be productive members of society.

To pursue being a mentor with Rupert's Kids, go to www.rupertskids.org, and click on the volunteers section. There is a form there to fill out to get things rolling!

Help Bring the Rupert's Kids Vision to your Community

The Rupert's Kids template can work in ANY community. All it takes is some dedication, hard work, and some mentors to jump start the program. With help from Rupert starting the program, you too can make a difference in your community. Help us show corporate America that it can profit by investing in the community and our program! We are building a nationwide database of partners to take our vision across America. To bring the program to your community, go to our website at www.rupertskids.org.

About the Writer

Lester Thomas Shane

Lester Thomas Shane's work as a writer, actor, and director has been seen on television, film, the New York stage, and in regional theatre.

For A&E Network Television's popular *Biography* series, Lester wrote *James Brown: Godfather of Soul, Tyrone Power: The Last Idol,* and *Carmen Miranda: The South American Way.* For AMC he wrote, *20th Century Fox: The First Fifty Years*; and for the Discovery Network, *Nazis: The Occult Conspiracy.* Lester is the co-author of several screenplays including *Pajama Party Horror, Nothing To Lose,* and *Portrait of the Artist As A Dead Man.* A series of his plays for children was published by Sundance. He co-developed the program, *P.O.V. Max* for The Children's Television Workshop. Lester has been a contributing writer for *A&E Monthly Magazine* and *Facilities.* With Penelope Brackett he wrote *Seven Keys to Success Without Struggle,* now in its second edition.

Lester is on the faculty of New York's American Academy of Dramatic Arts, and a member of the New Actor's Workshop, and the TADA! Ensemble.

Index

Index

A

H

I

K

S

T

U

V

W

Y

Z

Miracle Morning is AWESOME!

cute Kitty!